MIRACLES
FROM THE DUST

*God's power to heal revealed
through the life of an
Australian outback preacher*

John Mellor
with Rowena Beresford

MY wife Cathy and I first met John in Townsville in the early 1990s, where we attended the Christian Outreach Centre together. Even then, John impressed us as a man who had been radically saved and who had a strong personal relationship with his Saviour. One night, while praying, John shared with us a word of knowledge he had received from God about me.

I had been going through a series of personal setbacks, yet John said he could see me in a position where I was high up and that there were many people looking up to me. At the time, that seemed not even remotely attainable, however I have gone on to become Leader of the National Party in NSW. Looking back, John's vision was incredibly accurate.

We have stayed in touch and I now know that the incredible anointing that John has been given is being used by God in miraculous healing around the world. John's gift and his service in God's work have come at a personal price, but John continues to surrender his will to his Saviour. John's story is both fascinating and inspirational.

Andrew Stoner MP
Member for Oxley
Leader of The Nationals (NSW)

WITH so many books to read, autobiographies would have to be the most empowering resources available. John Mellor has written this book as a demonstration of his faith, hope and love in Jesus Christ. What stands out the most to me is his love for his family and for God.

When the world seemed to be collapsing around him, John said to his children, "Watch what God will do". As he remained accountable to the Word of God and His appointed leaders, God graced John with the gift of "miracle worker" and since then signs and wonders have been evident in every meeting.

This book will encourage you to believe for your own miracle, be it in your family, health or ministry.

Dr Chas Gullo
Queensland State Chairman, Christian Outreach Centre
Senior Pastor, Suncoast College & Church
Author

Artwork by: Kerry Stacey, Production Works
Cover photo by: Paulus Rusyanto
Printed by: Dominie Press, Singapore

ISBN 0-97755-380-9

A SPECIAL THANK YOU

Thank you to Scott Maloney for the interviews he conducted in the
Northern Territory which contributed to this book.

IMPORTANT DISCLAIMERS

The testimonies of miracles told in this book are based on my recollection
of the statements made by the people themselves. Although many have
verified the results with their doctors (particularly those that were written
up in newspaper articles), I make no claim about the veracity of their
statements, and base the stories of their healings solely on my recollection
of the words they themselves have spoken, and/or the words of those who
attended the meetings and/or witnessed the incidents occurring.

Included in this book are excerpts from a number of newspaper articles.
Please note that although the media often calls me a faith healer, I make
no claim to be one and in fact refute this completely. I am a Christian
evangelist who believes in the healing power of God. It is God and God
alone who heals. His power operates through my faith and obedience. My
only desire is to give glory to our Saviour for what He has done.

Aboriginal people in the Northern Territory related the information to me
that has been included in this book regarding aboriginal customs. Please
note that this has not been verified in any way.

Contents

FOREWORD 9
by Dr Linda Mason

INTRODUCTION 11
by John Mellor

CHAPTER 1 19
The Place of Small Beginnings

CHAPTER 2 41
Miracles from the Dust

CHAPTER 3 69
The Outpouring Begins

CHAPTER 4 101
The Fire Spreads

CHAPTER 5 125
A Prodigal Returns

CHAPTER 6 149
Challenges & Triumphs

CHAPTER 7 167
His Goodness Never Ends

NOTES 177

There are many people I would like to thank for their contribution to my life and ministry. These are just some of those people.

THANK YOU TO:

Glynda McNaught, for first recognising and encouraging the call on my life.

Terry Petersen, who challenged me, helped me work through some of the dysfunctions in my life and really stirred my heart for the lost.

Merv Westbrook, who was instrumental in expanding my effectiveness as an evangelist.

Kevin Dales, who has influenced me more than any other man in my life.

Kevin Wallis, who stirred me to believe that God still heals.

Crawford and Sheila Kirkwood, pastors of the Wishaw Christian Outreach Centre (Gateway Fellowship) for inviting me to Scotland, recognising the healing gift on my life and making a way for thousands of lives to be changed and healed.

Ashley Schmierer, who encouraged me and opened doors in Australia by sharing what he had seen happening in the UK.

Chas Gullo, who has helped me through more recent challenges in my life, and who provides spiritual covering and wise counsel for me as an individual and for this ministry.

I appreciate everything you have done and continue to do and know that God placed each of you in my life for His divine purpose.

by Dr Linda Mason

J esus said you "will do even greater works than these"[1]. He also said "preach the gospel and heal the sick"[2]. What did He mean by that?

In Christian history there has been a fairly strong tradition of Christian Medical Missions, but Jesus did not say "become doctors". There is nothing wrong with medical missions. I was a medical missionary doctor myself and believe that it is a great opportunity to serve people in the name of Jesus. However, when Jesus spoke those words, that's not what He meant.

The Bible tells us to "lay hands on the sick and they shall recover"[3]. I have seen this happening first-hand through John Mellor's ministry. Furthermore, I experienced it for myself.

When I first met John in July 2000, I'd been suffering from ME/CFS (chronic fatigue syndrome) for more than four years. He had recently arrived from Australia and was taking a small home group in Scotland. My friend Liz had invited me to go, as John was said to have a healing ministry. I was a bit sceptical, having tried all sorts of things to recover from ME. Even after John prayed for me, although I thought I felt a bit better I didn't know for sure whether anything had happened and was not going to believe anything too soon. I am trained to be scientific after all!

However, the days to follow were totally amazing. Instead of having to spend hours every day in bed, and feel exhausted if I so much as dusted one room, I was able to go jogging. I swam 500 metres with my son and even had a go at the gym. It was fantastic! People who knew me well could scarcely believe it.

I started going to John's regular Friday evening meetings hosted by the Christian Outreach Centre in Wishaw and took others with me who had seen the miracle God had done for me through John's ministry. I enjoyed being able to tell others about how God had healed me. There was such blessing in these meetings. My walk with God deepened and many times I would be overwhelmed with a sense of the tremendous love of God.

It was incredible to see miracles happening right in front of my eyes. One old lady whose hand was very deformed with rheumatoid arthritis was able to open up her hand for the first time in years. Her family wept as she threw away her sticks and walked around the meeting room.

Others testified as to how after prayer they had been delivered from depression, anxiety and alcoholism.

This book is full of stories like this. All I can say is, read on!

Dr Linda Mason
MB, ChB, MRCGP

by John Mellor

Since February 2000, I have travelled the world almost continually, preaching the gospel of Christ and praying for the sick everywhere from Australia to the USA, South America, Europe, Eastern Europe, Asia and Africa.

In every country, God has done incredible miracles time and time again. I have witnessed deaf ears hearing and blind eyes seeing. In fact, just recently, a 56-year-old woman who was born with one eye completely blind and had been told by doctors she would shortly be blind in the other, came to a meeting and had her sight completely restored. Other diseases like multiple sclerosis (MS) and fibromyalgia, which medicine has no answers for, have also been healed completely and wheelchairs cast aside as their occupants run around the room!

Numerous national and regional newspapers have published accounts of phenomenal healings. Television stations, such as Channel Seven in Australia, have broadcast stories and the BBC will be including a segment in a program scheduled for late 2007.

In August 2006, I was interviewed on Channel 25 (Canal 25) in the Dominican Republic and one of the studio cameramen asked me to pray for him during a break. Instead, I prayed for him live on camera, so the whole nation could see God do an amazing miracle. As the nation watched, the cameraman was dramatically healed of a painful leg injury he had suffered from for five years. The program was so popular it was broadcast again the following week.

Just recently, in Denmark, untold lives were changed and it would be impossible to relate everything that the Lord has been doing. People have been delivered and healed from many different diseases and sicknesses. Backs, shoulders, legs and heads have been set free from pain. Depression and fear have gone.

Many hundreds of people have made a commitment to give their lives to Christ and this has by far been the most exciting thing. Salvation remains the greatest miracle of all!

To give you just one example of the types of things that happened in Denmark, the neighbour of a pastor from the Cultural Centre in Copenhagen where I was preaching received an incredible miracle. This woman had bleeding on the brain, which had caused her to lose the ability to speak, and she could only communicate by slowly typing the words into a pocket computer. She also suffered tinnitus (ringing in the ears) and partial deafness. The Lord set her free after a number of prayers and her voice was released. Not only was she able to speak normally, but her ears were also healed! When she testified at church the following day it was hard to believe she had been dumb as she spoke perfectly and found it hard to stop.

I share these true stories to show you that there is no doubt God heals today, just as He did 2000 years ago when Jesus walked the earth.

Not everyone I pray for gets healed, and of those that do,

not all are instantaneous. Some people wake up the next day and their lives have changed, others see improvement over a period of time. Some never receive the healing they have come looking for. However, without a doubt, I see God move with power in every meeting, touching and changing lives.

Even as this introduction is being written, more miracles are occurring on an almost daily basis. Earlier this year, *Today Tonight*[4] broadcast the story of a four-year-old boy whose mother was told he would never walk, talk or be able to feed himself. He could only drag himself along the ground in an awkward seated position. Within a couple of weeks after I prayed for him at a meeting and asked God to heal him, he started walking. Now he is running around like any other four-year-old and chatting away happily. This miracle has caused a sensation across the country.

A more recent *Today Tonight* program featured a man who had been unable to walk for almost 10 years. The Lord healed him and he walked out of his wheelchair. While this story was broadcast across the nation, the untold miracle was even greater. This man was also blind and at the same time took off his sunglasses and cried, "I can see, I can see!".

In every country I visit, there are usually two questions I get asked. The first, "Where do you live?" is easily answered, although many people think I am joking when I tell them that I don't really live anywhere and that my suitcase is my home. Australia is, of course, my home in as much as I have one, but the reality is that I have no base, even though I am under the spiritual oversight of a church on the Sunshine Coast of Australia. I continually travel from one place to the other to preach the gospel.

The second question is usually something like, "How did this all begin?". This question requires a somewhat longer answer, which is where this book comes in. It is an attempt to tell this amazing true story of how someone like me has ended up crisscrossing the globe, continually seeing amazing miracles and hearing first-hand stories of how God has changed people's lives.

To be honest, my background was a mess and my family dysfunctional. My father was verbally abusive, angry and usually drunk, until in later years he found a relationship with God and was reconciled to us. My mother was raised in an institution and found it hard to adjust to the strains of life, suffering one nervous breakdown after another. My earliest memories are of spending time in the Red Cross Children's Home at Redcliffe in Queensland, and of our chaotic, anger-filled home.

At the age of 15 I stared drinking, finding the alcohol a useful anaesthetic to dull the pain of my troubled life. By 17 I was an alcoholic and became involved with different gangs. I became known as "Froth" after one day taking to my brother Jeff with a carving knife in an attack so serious that my friends later said I was "frothing at the mouth". At one stage I was also a "nominee" for an outlaw motorcycle gang, although thankfully I didn't go through with the dreadful initiation necessary to become a fully-fledged member.

At 18 I moved in with a girl and soon became a father for the first time. Our brief union was marked by great turmoil, largely due to my alcoholism, incredible anger and unstable nature. I was incapable of managing my own life, let alone anyone else's, and at that time was not a fit partner or parent. However, I will never regret the birth of Darren who is the result of that relationship. He is both my son and my friend.

A serious head-on collision caused me to remember four simple words my brother Jeff had spoken to me. Jeff had been delivered from drug addiction after attending Teen Challenge and soon after he told me, "John, hell will be forever". This moment was to be pivotal, but it wasn't until I was 20 that I finally gave my life to Jesus.

I was such an unlikely convert that when the minister heard what had happened he found it difficult to believe I wasn't playing another game. He was too intimidated to come and speak with me because I had been so aggressively anti-Christian. However, eventually even he could see that I really had encountered Jesus.

Shortly afterwards I met Joy and just over a year later we married. Within four years we had four young children: Jasmine, Jamin, Joel and Jonny.

In my early years as a Christian, I struggled with depression and found life difficult to cope with. Filled with cynicism and disbelief, at times I felt overwhelmed. But gradually God's power and the prayers and support I received brought healing to the many broken areas of my life.

One thing that has become clear to me is that God doesn't ignore the prayers of His saints even if it takes some time to see people change. I found out some years ago that the first person to hold me was Phyllis Cilento, who was the mother-in-law of the actor Sean Connery (probably best known as James Bond). Dr Cilento was a Christian and, according to those who knew her, prayed over the children born into her hands. She was actively involved in helping underprivileged families and did what she could to assist our troubled family. Right from the moment of my birth God had His people praying over me.

At the age of two, because of the ongoing problems in our family, I experienced my first stay in the Red Cross Children's Home. You can imagine how I felt when a few years ago I met a woman at one of my meetings who had been a nursing sister at the home. We got talking and I discovered she had been in charge of the small children at the very time I was there. She is a woman who loves God and she told me how every night she had prayed over the toddlers in her care, asking God to keep them safe and that they would come to know Him.

I also discovered that I come from a strong godly heritage. My forebears, the Stewarts of Bald Hills, were Scottish Christians who emigrated to Australia. Their sons were missionaries used by God to spread the gospel and one even helped to establish the fledgling Brisbane City Mission, which is still going today. Another was a missionary to the Aborigines. It is incredible to think that despite the difficult twists and turns their descendants have been through, God has been so faithful and called me to spread His word.

Although there is so much I could tell of the intervening years, this book primarily focuses on the period between 1994 and 2001. It starts with how my family and I moved to Katherine in the Northern Territory of Australia, telling the story of what God did in and through us as we worked with the indigenous people in the outback. It goes on to describe how Scotland played a key role in the river of healing that has been flowing ever since. From the red dust of the outback, and the dust of my broken life, God truly has brought amazing miracles.

My hope is that as you read this true story it builds your faith to believe that God can and does heal today. Not because of me, or any other pastor, preacher, or believer with faith to lay hands on the sick, but because He truly is the God of the miraculous. As it says in Hebrews 13:8, *Jesus is the same, yesterday, today and forever.* The miracles He did in Judea, Damascus, Galilee and Samaria 2000 years ago are still available today, for those who believe. I see them happen almost every day.

CHAPTER ONE

The Place of Small Beginnings

I don't think you could find a more unlikely location to start a ministry than Katherine. It is a place where people go to hide—to close a door on their previous life, hoping that it will never be reopened. This hard, hot and dusty outback town is more likely to be the burial ground of ministries than their birthplace, yet it was here that God chose to test me and open my eyes to the miraculous.

Katherine is a pretty wild place, with a relatively small population. In the days when we first went there only about 10,000 people called it home, even though it was the main regional centre for an area of land so vast that it is 35 per cent larger than England, Northern Ireland, Scotland and Wales combined!

The scenery is rugged and not very pretty, although it has its own wild beauty. Gum trees are stunted from lack of water and the ground is rocky and sparse. This is the true outback of Australia, with landscapes that vary from one extreme to the other—from barren desert where the aboriginal people are still following many of their tribal traditions, to the majesty of the Nitmiluk Gorge with incredible waterfalls and swimming holes and 200,000 tourists a year.

For six months of the year there is no rainfall at all. Then in the wet season it is unbearably hot and there is virtually a mass exodus of everyone (except the aboriginals) who can get out of town. They head south, go on holidays—whatever it takes to get away from the unbearable heat. Only those with air conditioning are willing to stay in Katherine during the wet season.

In 1994 we were living in Townsville, Queensland, when our church pastor, Kevin Dales, asked us to move to Katherine to pastor the Christian Outreach Centre (COC) church there. This opportunity was really the culmination of 10 years of preparation.

Back in the early 1980s we had spent four difficult but amazing years with Pastor Terry Peterson and his wife Kathy at Caboolture Christian Family. I think Joy's words sum up those years the most clearly. Reflecting back on that time, she described how I "arrived there in burnout and spent the four years there becoming human". Terry was incredibly influential in my life and instrumental in helping me work through the difficulties of my childhood. By the time we left there to move to the Queensland country town of Dalby (with their blessing), I was preaching and Joy was involved in the music ministry. Although we still had our troubles, we were different people because of that time of healing and restoration and the investment the Petersons made in our lives.

Moving to Dalby provided me with a teaching job and also meant the twins would be able to attend a Christian school, something we had been hoping and praying for. After about one year of teaching Pastor Merv Westbrook began releasing me from the school so that I could step into pastoral visitation. We got involved with children's programs, something both Joy and I loved, and eventually I started preaching. Merv was instrumental in planting satellite churches and we worked with him to start churches in Goondawindi, Chinchilla, Roma, Mundubbera and Oakey. Every weekend we loaded up at 4.30am and drove for about three hours until we reached whichever town we were scheduled to minister in with Merv that week. Eventually, we ran the Oakey church on our own each Sunday afternoon.

It was during a church prayer meeting that we first heard that the COC pastors in Katherine, Geoff and Isabel Warcon, were finding the incredibly pressured spiritual conditions there challenging. Joy and I couldn't stop thinking about them or praying for them. We longed to go to Katherine on a short-term trip and eventually, during the Christmas break of 1988/1989, we were able to do so. We spent seven weeks there, running children's programs and outreaches and doing whatever else we could to support the Warcons.

Not long after we returned from that trip, Pastor Merv let us know he was moving to Darwin[5], and that there would only be a voluntary position left in Dalby for me. I had heard that a teacher was needed in Townsville and, with the doors in Dalby rapidly closing, thought it would be a good idea to check it out.

We decided to move to Townsville with the idea that after 12 months we would look at whether the time was right to go to Katherine more permanently and help the

Warcons build the church there.

After the busyness of Dalby—where for two years it seemed we had returned home only to eat, sleep and change clothes—we needed the time at Townsville to recover. Kevin Dales, our new pastor, was fantastic. To give you an idea of what Kev is like, at one stage he closed down all the mid-week meetings because there was too much going on and told everyone to go home and invite each other over for dinner!

During the last 12 months of our time there, Kevin constantly did things to try to break his congregation out of religiosity and religious traditions (including Pentecostal ones)! At one stage he stacked up all the chairs and took them out of the church so there was nowhere to sit. That was one thing that really broke things open, because instead of sitting in little rows people went up the front and worshipped for hours. Church became a place that no-one wanted to leave to go home. At times, when the preaching was over the congregation would stay and just sit there. Sometimes there was no preaching and we just worshipped for the whole meeting.

If this had been done at the wrong time it would have had a negative effect, but the church had been praying for revival for months and it was definitely divine timing. Things were breaking open. In fact, we were at church one night when the fire brigade turned up because the neighbours had reported seeing tongues of fire on the roof! The Holy Spirit was really moving.

During this time I went on a ministry trip with Kevin and his wife Bev to Vanuatu. I had an overwhelming fear of flying so that was challenging, but the trip was absolutely life changing. It was my first overseas trip and my first overseas outreach. I saw the fire of God come on the meetings there. When we came back, I wanted to return with Joy and our children to do a long-term missionary trip. So much so that I continually harassed Kevin to agree! Eventually, Kevin, who was concerned about how we would survive the intense spiritual conditions of Vanuatu, asked us to go to Katherine as pastors instead.

By this time we had put our dream of returning to Katherine aside, thinking the door had closed. The church had now been shut down for months, and becoming the pastors there had certainly never crossed our minds. Our desire had just been to go and help.

I had had an interest in the aboriginal people for many years. Different churches we were involved in used to reach out to them and I had also spent some time as the principal of the Independent Aboriginal and Islander Community School at West End in Brisbane. I had been hired in a last ditch effort to keep the school open. Thankfully, it is still going today.

There was no question that my heart was for the indigenous people, but my wife Joy and I were of two minds about Katherine—torn between reticence and excitement. We knew only too well what going there would mean. Our trip out there five and a half years before had shown us all too vividly how far Katherine was from the rest of civilisation.

Our main concern was how our kids would feel about it, and it was definitely challenging for them. They found it difficult to get used to the idea of a permanent move to Katherine, instead of the six-month trip to Vanuatu we had been planning, but the boys came around after a few days. It was much harder for Jasmine, who at 14 was very attached to her friends and was very upset at leaving Townsville.

At that time I had a really good job and our lives were much more secure than they had been around the time of our first trip to Katherine in 1988. Then we had sold any surplus items and headed off with hardly any money, ending up with just one tank of petrol in a vehicle that God had miraculously provided.

Every step of the way was by faith and to even make it to Katherine was a miracle. We ate potatoes and beans for seven weeks and then returned to our home in Dalby for many more weeks of no money and no wage. I kept working as a teacher for the little school attached to our church, but because of unpaid school fees they had no money left to pay me. All they could do was give us access to the pastor's vegetable garden, where Joy and I would gather extra food for the children. Family Allowance[6] provided us with just below 40 dollars per week, which we used to buy any absolute necessities.

Once again we sold most of our belongings but this time we bought a big trailer to move things in, and a caravan that was to become our home. We knew that once we got to Katherine we wouldn't be able to afford to rent a house for at least a few months. The six of us headed off in two cars with all our worldly possessions hanging off the tow balls behind us and drove the 2200 kilometres from Townsville to our new home.

When we arrived in Katherine we didn't waste any time getting our church off the ground. Pastor Jeff and Isabel Warcon, who we had worked with on our last trip, had been gone for some time, and the pastor who succeeded them had also left. It had been eight months since the COC church was open in Katherine. Churches in the outback could go for up to five years without a minister or a pastor. It is so rough, remote and expensive that it is a hard place for a pastor and his family to survive.

We had the free use of a classroom in the local school and that was where we started our church. Each Sunday we moved all our equipment in, set it all up, and then took it home again at the end of the day. We started with just seven people and a lot of hope.

It wasn't long before five of those people had left. Soon after, the remaining two were also gone.

So there we were. Every Sunday we set up for church and started worshipping; I was the song leader and my wife and children made up the band. After the first few

> *"After the first few weeks [our] congregation consisted of just one person — and he wasn't exactly willing!"*

weeks of our ministry, which we had started so enthusiastically, the congregation consisted of just one person—and he wasn't exactly a willing participant!

We had been heading back to Katherine from a visit to Darwin when the pastor there asked us to allow Carl, a man who seemed beat up and battle weary, to travel with us. The few hours he spent in the car with us must have done something, because he began to feel sorry for us and when we got back to Katherine he started coming to our church. The only problem was we had a good old Pentecostal Holy

Spirit church and he had a Brethren background. At different times he walked out halfway through my preaching; my whole congregation just exited via stage left!

I often say I used to go and visit my congregation, but sometimes he wasn't home!

On one memorable occasion I got really excited. We received a phone call from a pastor in Darwin who told me about a young man who was moving down to Katherine. At that time he had only been saved for about six weeks. "You need him in your church, he is on fire for God", the pastor told me. "God has been doing a marvellous work in his life. He will be a real asset to your church."

The address he gave me was Unit 2 at the public hostel. I got really, really excited because it was so hard to get people into the church. Here was an opportunity to increase my congregation!

I rushed over there, charged up to the door, knocked and when the door opened, quickly said, "Hey mate, I am in a hurry. Get in the car, the service is going to start. We've only got about half an hour". After getting changed he came out and hopped into the car. We were driving along when I noticed that this man had a really mean look about him. He looked like the devil himself and he was growling at me. "Man," I thought to myself, "that pastor who told me he was saved, loved God and was on fire has no discernment at all!".

When we got to the church I said, "Hey mate, get up the steps the service is going to start". He went in and sat down and I started preaching with my usual enthusiasm. He just sat there with a dirty look on his face the whole time. As I looked at his expression, I thought to myself, "There must be something wrong; there is no way he can be saved!". Halfway through the meeting, another man walked in the door with a big smile on his face and sat down the back. I couldn't work out who it was, but it all became clear some time later when I found out that I had gone to the wrong door! After that day I never saw the man I had virtually kidnapped or the new convert again. The plan to expand our congregation had failed miserably.

By this time we had moved out of the school into the second floor of an old government building on the main street. It was dirty and horrible. We did our best to tidy it up but it wasn't very good. I talked the congregation into contributing, and he agreed to help me clean it.

The town drunks usually hung around the church because we had biscuits after the service. They would come and sit down, longing for the meeting to finish so they could eat the morning tea. Often the congregation consisted of just a handful of drunken old cowboys and a few aboriginals. It wasn't exactly an auspicious start to our ministry but it was a start.

To practise my preaching I went into the paddocks and pretended that the kangaroos were my congregation. It quickly became obvious to me that my sermons needed some work because every time I called out "rcpcnt, rcpcnt", the kangaroos hopped away. I wasn't left completely on my own, however, as Archie, our pet kangaroo, would follow me like a shadow. Archie also accompanied us to church, sometimes nestling in a pouch around my neck as I preached the Word.

We worked hard and very slowly our church grew. The closest aboriginal community to Katherine was Binjari, which was about 20 kilometres out of town, and we began to have outreach meetings there on Saturday evenings. On Sunday mornings we held our usual service. Later on in our ministry, I would also go to the School of the Air and use their facilities to broadcast Church of the Air. We have no idea how many people listened to our broadcasts because, from memory, only one family ever responded to us. Their story is quite incredible and if they are the sole reason God had us ministering to our "radio-wave" congregation it was well worth it!

Joe Wilson[7] and his family lived in the extreme northeast of Arnhem Land in the Northern Territory.

Joe was a man who worked hard. The aboriginal council employed him full-time as manager of Ramingining Station, which they owned. To supplement his income he also had a license from the government to collect crocodile eggs. At that time, it was illegal to hunt crocodiles in the wild, so the government licensed certain people to collect their eggs (subject to a quota). This allowed the crocodiles to be raised for their skins and I suppose it also helped keep the wild population down.

Crocodile egg harvesting is a very dangerous profession but the eggs bring in a lot of money, so Joe and his mate worked out a way to do it using his friend's helicopter. They would fly over crocodile infested areas and winch Joe out of the helicopter on a rope, holding a bucket in one hand and a revolver in the other. After he was lowered down from the helicopter, he would put the bucket down and locate a nest. Then he very carefully collected the eggs in one hand while his revolver was cocked and ready in the other. This was extremely dangerous, as crocodiles are naturally very protective of their nests.

As well as crocodiles, the remote area of the Territory that Joe was located in is full of wild buffalo. Joe was raised in the bush and his skills are probably almost as good as an aborigines'. This inspired him to start a business taking big game hunters from all around the world out on five-day safaris. They would travel into the most remote areas, full of danger and adventure, and hunt these huge buffalo.

On one very memorable occasion, Joe and an American hunter were camped by a billabong[8]. Each evening they made camp and in the morning Joe would walk down the slope to the water's edge, bend down and fill his billy[9] with water so they could make tea. Naturally, this is something he had done during many previous trips.

As an experienced bushman, Joe knew that crocodiles normally watch you for a while before they attack. When animals go down to the water to drink, a crocodile will usually lie hidden in the water, taking time to judge their prey. They are very patient and will often not attack until the fourth or fifth time that the animal comes to drink. This knowledge had previously kept him safe, but unfortunately it would not this time.

As Joe leaned across a pandanus tree to lower his billy into the water, a croc leapt up out of the billabong and grabbed him. With its jaws clamped onto his arm, it began dragging him into the water, intending to use the death roll[10] to finish him off. Joe hung on to the pandanus tree with all his strength, engaged in a bizarre tug-of-war with the croc. Hearing Joe screaming, the American came running down to the billabong to see what was going on and Joe yelled, "Shoot, shoot!". The hunter quickly fired his gun and as the shot hit the crocodile, it opened its massive jaws and let go of Joe's hand. Looking down in shock, Joe saw that his hand was almost completely severed and he was bleeding profusely. As he climbed the embankment away from the billabong the American saw the stump of Joe's arm, and almost fainted.

The area they were in was so remote they couldn't even use the radio. Joe was in a pretty bad way but he still had enough sense to grab a strip of something and use it as a tourniquet to stop the bleeding. In the meantime, the American was almost hysterical. Joe had to tell him to shut up and get in the car while he got behind the wheel.

"Joe's hand has been almost completely severed in a crocodile attack!"

It took three or four hours of driving through this remote and dangerous area before they made it to the nearest settlement at Bulman Station. Thankfully, there was a nurse on duty and Joe had called ahead as soon as the radio came into range, to warn them he was coming in. The nurse contacted the Flying Doctor[11] who flew to Bulman Station to meet them.

It was at this point that we came into the story. Joe's wife rang us when she found out what had happened and asked us to pray. She told us where Joe was and that his hand had been almost completely severed in a crocodile attack. He needed a miracle so I called the church to prayer.

All that was left of Joe's wrist was a small strand of flesh and sinew. The nurse severed his hand completely, cutting through that last connecting flesh, and placed it on ice in an

Esky[12]. They flew Joe and his severed hand to Darwin for emergency microsurgery in the hope of reattaching it. A team of specialists operated for quite a few hours, but the doctors weren't very hopeful due to the number of complicating factors. Because his hand had been torn off by the crocodile's teeth the wound was jagged and uneven, filled with all the germs and filth from the animal's mouth. To compound the problem, he was in the tropics and the wound had been exposed to the air for six or seven hours and had only been on ice for the last couple. After successfully sewing his hand back on, the doctors gave him a five per cent chance of ever getting any feeling or movement back in his hand.

As fantastic as they are, doctors are no match for our God, who is able to do anything. The church prayed fervently and within a short period of time, Joe had regained full use of his hand. All that was left to remind him were some pretty interesting scars, a few minor numb spots and some fairly incredible memories. The doctors were amazed. It was truly a miracle! Joe's story made the front page of the Darwin newspaper and the *Reader's Digest* quickly zeroed in. They offered him money to tell his story, but Joe, a shy man, wasn't interested.

To widen our reach, after the Church of the Air broadcast each Sunday, I hosted a Christian program on the local Katherine radio station, playing Christian music, telling stories and preaching five-minute messages.

Financially, life was very difficult. There was no support from the church or our denomination, of course, but we had a pioneering attitude that we were carving something out for God. We didn't resent the situation but at the same time it made life hard and put a lot of pressure on us.

In the meantime, our four youngest children (Darren had not come to Katherine with us) were making this rough outback town their home. Joel and Jamin eventually became stockmen and bull-riders and at times worked on remote outback stations mustering cattle.

With the help of Jasmine and Jonny and, I have to admit, some assistance from their mother and I, they also did their best to turn our home into a menagerie! On one occasion, Jamin raided a crocodile nest and planted the eggs in our garden. When they eventually started to hatch we had seven baby crocodiles on our hands and nowhere to put them except the bathtub. By this time nothing fazed us too much, although the same couldn't be said for our guests. Particularly when they met one of our pet snakes or bumped into a kangaroo hopping down our hallway!

About 10 horrible, difficult months went by before we could tell our church was making headway. Thankfully, Kevin and Beverley Dales were a great encouragement to us during this challenging time and towards the end of that first year Kevin reminded me that the only way to break through is by prayer and fasting. We decided to act on this wisdom and Joy and I started praying and fasting for the first 10 days of each month.

We were still doing a weekly outreach in Binjari—something we continued to do for much of the five years we were in Katherine—and it was there that I first saw someone get healed in response to my prayers. I can still vividly remember it. The meeting was like any other and, as per usual, people weren't really paying attention. It was obvious they found it all a bit boring, and most of them were playing cards with little interest in what we were doing.

Elsie was different. She was from the Wadaman tribe, an old lady with a broad smile that showed off her toothless gums. Elsie didn't speak English very well, but was fluent in Creole and her tribal language. I couldn't understand her and she couldn't understand me, but every Saturday Elsie and three or four kids would come to our outreach in Binjari where I told Bible stories, often acting them out so they could understand. There were no seats, which didn't bother them. They just sat on the grass and listened.

On this particular day Elsie came in as usual, limping on her bad leg, but for some reason I got really stirred up. I had personally been praying and fasting 10 days a month for five months by this time and I very strongly sensed that God wanted me to pray for Elsie to be healed.

To be honest, I wasn't really someone who believed in healing. My one and only experience had involved my son Jamin, who had been almost unable to speak until two American evangelists—Dave Roberson and Grady Miller—prayed for him when we were living in Caboolture.

Jamin, who at that time was just five years old, could say less than 10 words and even those words couldn't be understood by anyone other than his family. Joy and I had been praying for him for years and he had also had 12 months of speech therapy, yet there had been no improvement in his condition. We explained the situation to Dave and Grady and as soon as they started praying they bound a deaf and dumb spirit. By the time we got home that night he was speaking! Over the years I had seen many people prayed for and yet, as far as I can recall, this was the only time I had seen someone get healed like this.

With such a lack of experience, I wasn't exactly used to asking people to come forward for prayer, but I knew that was what God wanted me to do. Elsie's kids translated my request and in response she shuffled to the front and I laid hands on her leg and prayed that the Lord would heal her. After the meeting, I didn't think much more about it.

The next week when we arrived we could tell something had changed—there was already a group of people waiting for us. This was the first time anyone other than Elsie and her kids had really shown any interest.

> *"We could tell something had changed ... I found out later that Elsie's leg had been healed."*

I found out later that Elsie's leg had been healed and word had quickly spread around the community about what had happened. A number of the aboriginals came out for prayer and more people got healed. Before you knew it, we were having a little revival. Many of the people stopped playing cards and drinking, and gave their lives to Jesus.

I prayed for people and God moved. There began to be real changes in the community. They stopped gambling and drinking and wanted to come to church. We shoe-horned as many people as we could into the small church bus each Sunday night and drove them to and from church. Our congregation was really first built on those Binjari people.

When people began to get healed it was slowly at first, one here, one there, a couple here, a couple there, and it was difficult for me to understand what was happening. I had never really seen any results when I had prayed for people before and wasn't too sure about it. That was in 1994 and, in spite of my uncertainty, other aborigines began to seek me out.

Because of my qualifications, I was able to go into the communities as a relief teacher. Back in those days, non-aboriginal people couldn't go on tribal land without a permit, so being a teacher gave me access to communities I

The Binjari people crammed into the church bus for a Sunday night meeting. The elderly lady in the far left of the picture is Elsie.

wouldn't have been able to visit otherwise. Teaching was one of the ways by which I was able to go in and share the gospel.

The government supplied petrol for the trips—which could take anywhere between six and 15 hours, depending on which community I was going to. They also paid my wages while I was there. I taught during my working hours and spent the evenings preaching and praying for the sick.

We had outreaches as far as Kununurra, Kalkaringi (which is out towards the West Australian border in the middle of nowhere), Ngukurr[13] and a lot of other places whose names I no longer remember. I often slept in the back of my car after dining on canned food, fruit and cereal.

God used these opportunities in an amazing way. I began to get more and more involved with a community called Wugularr in Beswick, about 150 kilometres outside Katherine and we started to see a real revival there. A large proportion of the community turned to Jesus and were filled with the Holy Spirit.

Around this time I went on a trip to Pensacola in the USA. During this trip God really touched my heart and I felt His power on my life. It spurred me on to want more of Him. Joy could see the change in me when I returned home.

The people in Wugularr were also hungry for more of God. Many people had sown seeds into their lives over the years, including missionaries and other church groups, and changes had been happening gradually, but it was God's timing and He moved sovereignly in their lives like a mighty river. We were blessed to witness what He did there.

Crime, drinking and petrol sniffing went down and there were visible changes in the way they lived. The gospel had a marked impact on this community.

Whenever I was preaching I could sense the power of God. As I sat around the campfire preaching the gospel, the Holy Spirit just came … it was incredible. Some of the most powerful meetings I have ever held were under the stars in the dry bulldust[14] of the paddock, rather than within the confines of a church building.

In the past the aboriginal people weren't formally educated like other Australians. It is only in recent times that education has become a real priority in the remote areas. Traditionally they would go wandering, commonly known as "going walkabout", which meant they missed out on a great deal of school time. They are a very spiritual people and in their traditions they have dreams, which are part of their communication with the spirit world. When they get

New Christians being baptised in the Wugularr community.

saved they still have dreams, but now they tell of Jesus and the angels, seeing revivals and dreaming of things that are so accurate and theologically sound they can't be denied as having come from God.

Dreams are also an important part of tribal law. For example, before a child is born the spirits show the father the child's totem in a dream. When they get born again and baptised in the Holy Spirit, they go from one spirit world to the other. It is a different spirit now but they are doing the same sorts of things—God gives them dreams and visions. The Bible talks about discernment of spirits and they are certainly able to discern them.

They can be sitting right in front of you and, without trying, see clearly into the spirit world. Often their descriptions of the spirits were so vivid that it was as if they were describing a flesh and blood person.

Many also told of God speaking to them in dreams. They would say things like, "God told me in a dream I have to stop smoking … God told me in a dream I have to stop mistreating my wife …". Even more significantly, they would obey what was said to them. I knew the dreams couldn't be coming from Satan as he does not give people dreams that cause them to stop doing evil and live righteously.

It is also common for the aboriginal children to have dreams and visions. Often they told me that Jesus had come and spoken to them the night before. When I asked what He looked like they described Him in words that sounded as if they came straight out of the book of Revelation, or Daniel, "… He had a white robe and eyes like fire …". These kids had never read the Bible but they described very intricately what they had seen and it all lined up with the Word. There was never anything that was doctrinally unsound.

As well as being very open spiritually, the aboriginal people are very demonstrative. Often—even when the person who had died did not know the Lord—the tribe would ask me to take the funeral. I have even conducted funerals for tribal elders who were still completely immersed in their culture. These were huge events that could have as many as 800 people present.

Their idea of a funeral is incredibly different to what white people are used to. They grieve, they scream, they cry. As a people they get their feelings out quickly—and loudly—so they can forget about them and move on, unlike most of us who hide our feelings and live a lifetime of grief.

> *"He had a white robe and eyes like fire …"*

On some occasions, the funerals began with their ceremonies. The aboriginals dressed up in their tribal gear and carried spears and clap sticks[15]. At times I witnessed them trying to cut and maim themselves with knives and scissors. The sounds of children screaming hysterically were often mixed with the unmistakably haunting sounds of the didgeridoo[16], as the children drew back in fear when it was their turn to lie on the coffin[17].

When the ceremonies were over, I would stand and speak about Jesus. In the midst of all this incredible howling and crying, a hush would fall over the people as Joy started singing. Nothing ever settled them down like the sound of her voice praising God. The local funeral director often sought her out, wanting her to sing at every funeral because of the calm it would bring over the people.

We took every opportunity God gave us to preach the gospel.

As I conduct a Christian funeral, a medicine man in traditional funeral attire curses the people and tries to call them back to the dreamtime.

CHAPTER TWO

Miracles from the Dust

While there were many who responded to the gospel, it wasn't all easy in the aboriginal communities. Many times when I went out to the remote regions to preach and teach I had to lock myself in the school office at night because that was the only safe place to sleep. Some offices were surrounded with an iron cage to secure the computers and valuables and at times those who had been drinking heavily would come and rattle the cage, yell at me or throw rocks at the roof, doing anything they could to harass me. I had to learn to just turn myself off, shut it all out and go to sleep.

I was an outsider. Usually just one of a handful of white people amongst hundreds of the local aborigines and the situation was potentially intimidating. Sometimes when I went to a community different ones who had been drinking would hurl abuse at me and even threaten to bash me. At other times when I was holding meetings in the field they came and knocked people down, or screamed out abuse: "I am going to kill you! I am going to get you …". They often staggered and fell, drunk, stoned or bombed out from petrol sniffing.

Then there were the camp dogs. Every time I had an altar call, asking people to come forward to accept Jesus as their Lord and Saviour, the camp dogs would attack people and howl. It was demonic. It seemed like they were always on the lookout for an opportunity. I was praying for a lady during one visit when I felt a sudden sharp pain in the back of my leg. Looking down I saw a dog with its jaws locked onto my ankle. On another occasion I was walking through the community praying, when a dog leaped out at me and ripped into my leg. Blood poured from where the teeth had punctured my skin and the pain was incredible.

I have held meetings where a pack of dogs ran through the gathering at a crucial moment, scattering people all over the place as they clambered to escape from these aggressive animals.

After experiencing what it was like to be bitten, I started carrying what I called a "camp dog stick", ready to fend them off if they tried it again. Many of the dogs, which were used for hunting, had dingo[18] in them and were pretty savage.

Later, when I took a mission team from the Brownsville Revival Bible College in the United States out to the community, I warned them, "Watch this. When you give an altar call and say 'the Blood of Jesus', the dogs are going to come in and try and scatter the people, but you take authority in the name of Jesus and don't let them do it". Sure enough, it happened. They told me afterwards they never would have believed me if they had not seen it for themselves.

Dogs, dirt, dust, campfires, drunks, fights, rape, petrol sniffing, more violence and even murder … these were some of the things we had to contend with in our outback ministry.

At one place a man picked up a spear, put it through a woman's neck and killed her. The next day when I arrived to conduct one of my very first meetings, the Christian aboriginals wouldn't allow me to preach because the people were naturally very upset. Traditionally, the aboriginals have a payback system and while I was there someone tried to kill the nephew of the murderer as punishment.

During an open-air meeting in Wugularr one of the girls was singing at the front when a man came out, grabbed the mike and smashed it into her face, knocking her onto the ground. In the middle of that I was trying to preach the gospel.

Even now tribal aborigines are still involved in all their rituals and ceremonies, and their corroborees. Some still point the bone and put curses on people[19]. The enemy tries to use this to stop what God is doing. Sometimes he succeeds

> *"Dogs, dirt, drunks, violence and even murder were some of the things we had to contend with …"*

in getting in the way, but there were many times we saw God's amazing hand.

That was particularly true during 1995, when Jason, a full-blood tribal aboriginal from Arnhem Land, became a Christian and joined our church. I began to train him up, to mentor and disciple him to become my right-hand man.

Jason has a heart for his people and he asked me to go out to the settlement at Ngukurr. The outreach was very successful and about 22 young men gave their lives to the Lord. Many were also healed and the people just couldn't stop talking about it.

The next time we went out there we took a man called Kevin Wallace with us. We sensed a really heavy atmosphere but didn't know why until Kevin returned from a walk saying, "Do you know what is going on over the other side?". He had seen the aborigines with their spears dancing around; they were having a corroboree.

Kevin Wallace was a real cowboy preacher and had a heart to see people get healed. A former Australian Rookie Bareback Champion, he and his wife, Lisa, had recently joined our church. Kevin and I used to stay up all night talking about miracles. We talked about travelling the world and going out and seeing revival.

> *"Next thing he started walking – moving his legs and walking!"*

I was with Kevin when I saw my first really profound miracle. We were doing another outreach at Ngukurr and I was preaching on how God can do anything. Although the people were usually very shy, they brought forward a man who had been paralysed for three years from a stroke. The Holy Spirit inspired me to tell him, "Jesus is going to heal you". Kevin started to pray for him and I laid hands on him too, but to be honest I think God moved more in response to Kevin's faith than mine! Kevin had been reading a lot of Kenneth Hagan books on healing and he was really praying for this guy. When Kevin asked how he was the man told us there was heat in his legs, and he could also move them a little. Kevin got him by the hands while I was still praying for his legs and pulled him up. Next thing he started walking—moving his legs and walking! I had never seen a paralysed man walk before. That stirred the people right up and that night we saw many miracles, many wonderful things.

At that time my Dad kept sending me videos of Benny Hinn but I really wasn't interested. However, with Kevin's encouragement I decided to watch just one of them. Before too long I got past his style—which was so very different from the world I lived in—and I began to see the reality of the miracles. I can remember thinking how amazing it all was.

So there I was—spending a lot of time with Kevin who had great faith and a real passion to see God's power move in people's lives, and also experiencing what was happening with the Binjari people as God moved amongst them. The amazing things I was witnessing helped me to appreciate Benny Hinn's ministry. As a result, my faith began to grow and so did our church. I saw more and more people get healed. It was wild! We often drove seven or eight hours to remote aboriginal communities just to hold one meeting. After preaching for hours and praying for the sick we would sleep in the school hall, or in the back of our vehicles, and then drive back home the next day.

Invitations poured in from everywhere. Sometimes we would go to Elliott, an aboriginal community about five hours south. On other occasions we went as far as Kununurra, eight or nine hours west of Katherine into the neighbouring state of Western Australia. I did a lot of sleeping in my car.

The man that was healed at Ngukurr came to my church at Katherine, walked up the steps and gave his testimony. He had a walking stick and was still a bit stiff in one leg, but considering he had been totally paralysed before, it was incredible. He was so thankful for what God had done for him that he wanted to publicly testify how Jesus had touched him. Seeing a miracle like this for the first time really stirred me up to believe for more.

It was during this time that I experienced one of those "God moments" you never forget. I often used to spend time on the banks of the Katherine River, praying and communing with God; I guess you could call it my "quiet place". On this particular occasion I was searching my mind, looking for a logical explanation for the incredible things that had been happening. After all, logic is so much easier than faith! For 16 years I had been a "sceptical Christian", analysing everything intellectually. I was full of unbelief and doubt and had been critical of anything supernatural. As I sat there, God very clearly spoke to me and said something along the lines of, "John, accept the healings and stop trying to work them out". He was clearly telling me that it was His hand I was seeing at work, something for which there is no "logical" explanation.

From then on, my trust in God increased considerably as I stopped trying to work it out in my head and just took Him at His Word.

When Kevin and I went to Binjari and prayed for a lady with a paralysed arm, God restored her and she could move her arm again. We saw a lot of wonderful things happen and driving along would pray and praise God, crying out, "Lord, we are believing that You will do an outstanding miracle tonight!". He always answered our prayers.

As the aboriginals cooked what was usually kangaroo,

shellfish, or goanna[20] on the campfire to share with us, I told them Bible stories about Jesus and taught them songs, picking out the tunes on an old guitar. The power of God always came. They lined up for prayer and sometimes there would be 50 people patiently waiting for God to move in their lives. We saw bones straightening, legs straightening, all kinds of phenomenal things … the Holy Spirit always seemed to come when we were around the campfire.

I remember praying for a man at Elliott who had been a pastor but had slipped back into their ceremonies. In some tribes if aboriginals don't attend ceremonies they offend and disobey their cultural laws and naturally this is quite a dilemma for them. For a Christian to really stand for God in those places they need courage because they come under a lot of pressure. This man began to go back to the ceremonies to please his people and he got involved in a mortuary ceremony.

"We saw bones straightening, legs straightening, all kinds of phenomenal things …"

Certain tribes believe that when someone dies the spirits transfer to another person, like a form of reincarnation. In a dream they will be shown the person the spirit is to transfer into; this could be another relative, a child, or someone else.

That person has to lie next to the dead person for seven days. Meanwhile there is terrible heat, the body is swelling, there are flies and naturally it stinks. Every day they conduct a mortuary ceremony, to transfer the dreamtime spirit from the dead person into the body of the live person.

This man was normal until, during the ceremony and the transfer of the spirits, he took a fit, fell to the ground and began to shake. He started burning with fever and became listless. They took him to the kadachi man (witch doctor) but he didn't know what was wrong with him. Neither did the local missionaries, or the white doctors. None of them could help him. He was at the camp at Elliott and, as we laid hands on him, the power of God touched him and set him free.

Kevin and I got a reputation in those days for helping those that no-one else could.

One day a white lady who had fostered an aboriginal child called me for help. The boy had gone to a mortuary ceremony and lain next to the body of his uncle for seven days. You can imagine how distressing that would be for anyone, let alone a child. Each day they conducted the ceremony and after seven days when that child came back into Katherine, he was behaving erratically. He became very violent, smashing things, screaming, and having nightmares. His foster mother had heard what we were doing, and that a lot of people who were tormented had been set free. Out of desperation she contacted us and I went and talked to the child. Then I went to the child's room and prayed, covering it by faith with the Blood of Jesus. Two days later the lady rang me to say that the child was fine and had been ever since I had prayed for him.

The Bible is very plain that there are two kingdoms— the kingdom of darkness and the kingdom of light. When you are dealing with these spirits, the Bible clearly states that if it is not of God it is from the darkness. Even their own witch doctors couldn't help those people, but when we cast the spirits out in the name of Jesus, they left.

Some tribal aboriginals are still involved in "cursing" each other, commonly called "pointing the bone". The cursed person often becomes listless and stops eating. However, when we prayed God set these people free. Dealing with spiritual issues like this became fairly common for us.

On another occasion my wife and I received a phone call at one o'clock in the morning from some distressed people in the Eva Valley, who had heard about this ministry. "We have a man who the spirits have got hold of," they told us. "He has thrown himself into the fire in an attempt to kill himself, screaming and tormented." We arranged to meet them at the church and they arrived at about four in the morning. The whole tribe of about 25 people brought him. His eyes were rolling and he had foam around his mouth; it was obvious that he was totally tormented. We laid hands on him and when the power of God hit him he fell on the floor and lay there in a trance. When he finally got up we could see that God had set him free.

The pressure for aboriginals to conform to their culture is incredibly powerful. Often they try to mix Christianity with their own culture, but the problem is that their ceremonies are actually worship, and it is not the God of the Bible they are worshipping.

In every culture, including that of mainstream Australia or any other nation, there are positives and negatives. It is important to hold onto those aspects of our culture that don't conflict with what God reveals to us, and exchange those that do for His truth.

When aboriginals get born again they often come under a lot of persecution. This happened with one of the aboriginals we knew. He went through everything from receiving death threats to having spears thrown at him.

In his tribe, when a child is about five years old, the uncle takes over responsibility for raising the child and teaches them the ways of the dreamtime, the aboriginal culture. But this man was a Christian and he didn't want his kids involved in the ceremonies of the dreamtime. They began to persecute him because he wouldn't allow them to take his boy away.

He wanted to get married and the elders got very angry with him, saying, "You don't get married, you do it by tribal law". But he wanted to get married in the eyes of God. They tried to give him alcohol, because if a person above you, a tribal elder, tells you to do something you have to obey. If they offer you a drink and you refuse it, they take it as an insult. They tried everything in an attempt to make him fall. On one occasion they held him down and began to pour alcohol down his throat. They threatened to kill him because he was going against all his tribal ways.

The persecution was so severe that he and his family had to get out. They fled to the city to escape the torment. During this time one of his children was hit by a car and died, but through all of this the family have held onto their faith in God.

During the time we spent amongst the aboriginals I began to learn more about what it is like to live in this day and age as a tribal aborigine. For example, under tribal law, if someone kills or injures another person—even accidentally—they have to pay for it. That is tribal justice. Sometimes that involves other tribe members driving a barbed spear through the offender's leg at a certain angle, which is designed to tear out the main tendons and leaves the person with a permanent limp.

The Australian government tries to walk a line between "white man's law" and "black man's law". If an aboriginal agrees to face tribal punishment they will generally receive a greatly reduced sentence under white man's law. Many of the indigenous people will choose to face both forms of punishment. They know that if they only face the law of the State they will still be forced to pay via tribal law one day, no matter how long it takes.

Tribal law is very brutal. One of Jason's uncles killed a man and for his punishment, he had to stand in one place while four or five men stood at a specified distance and threw spears at him. The police used to come and monitor the spearings to make sure they were carried out properly, because otherwise it would create more reprisals. After it was over, or any other tribal sentence had been carried out, the person would be free. The idea is to dodge the spears because if you can do that it proves you are innocent.

> *"He had to stand in one place while spears were thrown at him."*

Closer to the towns a lot of the tribal law has been broken down but it is still present to some degree. In the remote areas it continues to be very strong. We were working hard running our little church while also having to take these challenging realities into consideration.

Often when an aboriginal became a Christian we would try to help them break their addiction to alcohol. We lived nine kilometres out of town in a missionary's house, so this usually involved them camping in our backyard.

One night, while Joy and I were at a motel, having taken a rare night off to celebrate our wedding anniversary, the kids rang in a panic saying, "Dad, it's Cameron, he's trying to kill May. Come and help, come and help!". We rushed back home in time to see Cameron with an iron bar in his hand threatening his wife … it was just horrible. Joy ran straight over to him and I could see he was going to bring this iron bar down on her head. She just cried out, "Jesus, Jesus!".

I told him to put the bar down but he was wild from drinking. He came and stood over me and as he was about to drive his fist in to my face I cried out, "Jesus!". I could almost feel the force of the blow but it never connected. He just stood there for a few seconds and then backed off. We used to have these types of experiences fairly often and although they were incredibly stressful God always protected us.

Violence and even murder were just so common. When we were in Katherine one government authority informed us that the average lifespan for an aboriginal male was about 41, because of disease, violence, and poor diet.

There were two women in my church who had killed people by slicing their main artery, causing them to bleed to death. One of them was a Walpuri woman. Her husband used to get drunk all the time and he really attacked her. One day as he was doing this she grabbed a knife and sliced his thighs. As a result, she had to face tribal justice and a reduced jail sentence. This happened while she was in our church. The other woman had a fight with her brother and put a knife through his neck.

If a man suspects his wife of committing adultery he is likely to smash her femur (thigh bone) with a rock so she can't go anywhere. It wasn't uncommon for us to see women on crutches; their husbands would just break their legs. It was extremely brutal and almost every day there was some fresh outbreak of violence.

Actions like this could spark an almost never-ending cycle of aggression. One couple who were regular, committed members of our church were a prime example of this. When the husband went to the hospital to pick his wife up (after he had broken her leg), she waited until he was holding the taxi door open and then brought her wooden crutch down on his arm, instantly snapping the bone. Instead of going home, they had to let the taxi go and return to the hospital so the husband could have his arm set!

The way the aboriginals view death is also different. When someone dies they rarely believe it is due to natural causes. Instead they will look for a spiritual reason, such as a curse. If someone is in a car accident, they may not see it as a car accident, but rather believe that it happened because someone has put a curse on them. They will take something belonging to the person involved in the accident to the kadachi man, to find out who did it. He will supposedly tell them who was responsible and in turn they will either put a curse on that person or go and punish them (even if it isn't really true). The kadachi men have incredible power because of people's fear. The people believe whatever they say, because it is such a strong part of their culture.

We had to do a lot of praying for the aboriginal people when they got saved, especially people who had been "sung"[21] as they were usually dying. Tribal beliefs are very strong, but—praise God—Jesus is stronger!

On one memorable occasion Jason had gone out to Numbulwar, a place so wild they have been known to throw spears through shop windows. He was at a meeting when a man with a handful of spears threw one at Jason and his wife as they were worshipping and praying. Just as he did, a car came around the corner and deflected the spear so it didn't touch them. When the man who threw it saw what had happened, he knew that divine intervention had prevented his spear from reaching its target and broke down. Crying, he gave his life to Jesus.

Jason was full of faith right from the beginning and he often used to pray for the sick. Once when he was out in a remote community, there was a baby who was turning blue and was virtually without hope. They called the Flying Doctor over the radio, but in the meantime Jason went and laid hands on the baby and prayed for him, and he was healed.

Another time they were out in the bush hunting and a child who was with them became very ill and died. Jason told the people with him about the miracles of Jesus. When the father picked the child up he could see the baby had stopped breathing; it was dehydrated and there were no signs of life. By faith, the father gave the baby up to God and it began to breathe. That baby came back to life!

These stories are real. In the dust and dryness of the Australian outback, God was doing outstanding miracles.

We saw many amazing things but when I went to the annual church conference in Brisbane and tried to tell people what had been happening, they struggled to believe me. It seemed as if they thought I had been out in the bush for too long. After a while I decided to just keep quiet.

"… the father gave the baby up to God and it began to breathe."

Being pastors in Katherine wasn't like your normal Christian ministry, that is certain, but God was moving and we were doing everything we could not to get in His way. Our church was doing really well. People were getting saved and baptised, the congregation was slowly growing and it looked like things were finally coming together. The environment we were in was extreme, but God used it to strengthen my faith and enlarge me.

* * * * *

Then one Monday during the wet season of January 1998 everything changed. The day before it had started raining and hadn't stopped—not that there was anything unusual in that. We had a YWAM team ministering in church that Sunday and the following morning Joy was to do a number of trips to drive all 15 or so of them into town to catch the bus back to Darwin.

The first trip started at about 6.30am and at that time there was water running across the driveway to our house. We weren't too concerned until Joy came home on her third and final trip and told me that the river was rising much faster than usual. Each time she had gone past it had been another metre higher.

We moved our vehicles to higher ground just in case and in the meantime the river kept rising. By early evening it was

My son Jonny standing on the roof with our neighbour, watching the water rise.

up to about 16 metres[22] and we decided we had better move Joy's horses to higher ground before they got trapped. The rest of our considerable menagerie had to stay where it was for the time being.

We dropped halters over the horses' heads and holding on to those to lead them, waded through thigh-deep water to take them to the other side. By the time we were ready to cross back through, the water was considerably higher and we were battling to stay upright in the strong current. One of the halters became a lifeline for us, as we each held tightly to one end so we wouldn't be swept away from each other.

Things were looking very bad when we got back home and we slept only fitfully that night. At about two o'clock in the morning, our son Jonny woke us. The water was lapping at the concrete slab under the house.

By the time daylight came there was a considerable volume of water running through the ground floor of our house and it was still rising. To save our many animals, we decided to haul them up onto the verandah on the second story of our house. After a mammoth effort taking some hours, two poddy calves[23], a bush pig, some chooks, our sausage dog, our cat, a cockatoo, a galah[24] and two huge dogs belonging to our neighbours were safely installed.

The next-door neighbour's family of four had also joined us, as well as an English backpacker named Steven who had come to Katherine to see his estranged father and ended up staying with us.

By the time we got all the animals—and the people—upstairs all we could do was sit and watch the water continue to rise, until we had literally become part of the river and our house was like a small and vulnerable island in the midst of the raging torrent. The river that had been our playground and the scene of wonderful memories, particularly from our family camp-outs on the sandy banks most Friday nights, was unrecognisable.

Looking out, white knuckles grasping the verandah rails, there were sharp intakes of breath from each person standing there every time a huge log broke free from the riverbank. Tumbling down the whitewater rapids towards us, picking up so much speed that they hurtled forward like some horrific machine of destruction; each log was capable of smashing our little house to pieces.

> *"Our house was like a small and vulnerable island in the midst of the raging torrent ... "*

As the day wore on, and our stress increased, our minds were focused on what was going to happen that night. The water was still rising and we were in the midst of this huge, swollen and rapidly flowing river.

Incredibly, we still had a working telephone, even though our electricity, gas and water had long since been cut. When the State Emergency Services (SES) contacted us to ask if we would like to be rescued we jumped at the chance. At this stage the water was slapping against the house, just two steps below the second storey. The entire ground floor was submerged.

The only way we could be rescued was to climb onto the roof of the house, as there was nowhere for the helicopter to land. We would have to be winched up from there.

What do you take with you when you think you are

about to lose everything? All we could think of were family photos and videos, all our precious memories.

Joy started madly stuffing them all into a bag. We couldn't even think clearly enough to pack a scrap of clothing or any other practical items we might need. All we cared about were those things that couldn't be replaced.

Carefully, one by one, we climbed onto the corrugated iron water tank, not daring to look down at what was below us. From there it was a short climb to the roof. I can't begin to describe what it was like, standing on the roof of our house surrounded by water. All we could hear was the rushing sound of the river, the cries of the frightened animals and our own ragged breath. Eventually the tell-tale noise of the helicopter reached our ears as the chopper came closer and started hovering over the house, the wind from the rotor blades forcing the water to recede like waves rolling back from the house.

Because there was a very tall tree nearby, the helicopter could not come too close or it would be in danger from the tree branches. The SES lowered one of their team onto the roof along with a padded harness on the end of a cable. They had instructed us over the phone on how to pull the harness over our upper body like a lasso, until it was just below our arms. We were then to hold onto the cable above our heads as they pulled us up.

The boys went first and we helped each of them get the harness positioned properly. The winch was working overtime because of the long distance they had to haul the cable over. This caused the motor to start overheating and they were forced to drop our sons off on the only available patch of dry ground, a small sand hill poking out of the water nearby, to allow it to cool down.

Eventually they came back for the rest of us. It was incredibly nerve-wracking watching each person in turn dangling in the air above our heads, the tension showing on their faces.

After watching my family and neighbours being winched off the roof one-by-one it was my turn. Looking up, I could see the helicopter silhouetted against the grey sky and hear the incredible noise of the rotors. Soon I was in the harness and the signal was given. As I dangled above the swirling floodwaters, I was mesmorised by the view below me. An almost never-ending cargo of debris was being carried along by the swollen river and the extent of the destruction was clearly evident. For one strange moment in time as I was suspended in midair over this chaotic scene, I felt an amazing mixture of elation. I began to think about the world and its people and in that moment I knew that God was going to send me to the nations. The moment was over almost as soon as it began and I was pulled awkwardly into the hatch of the helicopter.

> " ... we were dangling above the earth, with nothing but a cable to hold us ... "

As Joy had been pulled into the helicopter she felt like it was on an angle and she was going to fall straight out again. She had a vice grip on the cable and passed out before they could eventually pry it from her hands. By the time I got into the helicopter, she had broken down and was crying desperately, terribly distressed at the thought that Noodles (our sausage dog) would be left on the roof zipped up in the backpack she had put him in. Thankfully the member of the helicopter crew who had been lowered onto the roof to supervise our evacuation was winched up after me and, breaking protocol, brought Noodles with him.

The stress of the situation was just unbelievable. We didn't know if we would ever see our home again.

In the meantime the boys were in trouble. A bull had been washed down the river and, taking up residence on the same small "island", had taken offence at their presence. While we were dangling above the earth with nothing but a cable to hold us, they were dodging a crazed bull that was trying to force them into the water.

As the helicopter carried us into town we could clearly see the damage to the surrounding landscape. The river was raging and the power lines had fallen, ringing out each time they slapped against the surging water with a sound almost like a gunshot. The caravan park next door where we had lived when we first came to Katherine was completely submerged and there were rapids wiping out everything in their path. Demountable buildings and caravans were scattered and overturned and there was refuse everywhere. I had never seen anything like it in my life.

As we flew into town we realised that most of Katherine was also under water. Very few people had evacuated, or even saved their most valued possessions. The radio broadcasters had been telling them to evacuate all day but no-one believed that the water would rise above the "100-year flood level" signposted in town. Even at that level, they knew their homes were safe. But the water rose much, much higher and people lost everything. They didn't move their cars when they had a chance. They didn't save their photos. In most cases all they escaped with was their lives. Tragically, four people weren't that fortunate.

It was another week before the water went down enough to let us go back to the house and pick up a few essential belongings. But it was another couple of weeks before we had water and power and could actually go home. There was a food line at Katherine East and everyone from rich to poor—both white and aboriginal—was there. We were all equal in that situation—a natural disaster of this magnitude is an incredible "leveller".

Families who hadn't been flooded took in those who had and were just as distressed by the situation; they felt incredibly guilty over still having everything when so many no longer had anything.

For us personally there was more to come. Political things were happening in the broader church hierarchy relating to our church and ministry in Katherine that we just couldn't, in all conscience, agree with. Within one week after the flood we found ourselves in a position where it felt like our backs were in a corner and there was no option left but to resign. It was one of the most difficult things I have ever had to do. We were persuaded to hold on but finally, several months later, had to go through with our resignation.

Our church just cried when it happened. They loved us and things had been going so well after all the hard work we had put in.

At that time the minister of another church in town gave me the opportunity to be an unofficial Associate Pastor so I went over there. Joy no longer wanted to be involved in the ministry. Looking back, Joy says she just felt the overwhelming need to be a normal person.

I didn't realise then that we were both suffering the effects of post-traumatic stress. We had had this incredible rescue by helicopter after spending two days not knowing whether we would be washed away at any moment. The bottom floor of our house was flooded; we were living like refugees and trying to help deal with the incredible losses to our town and its people. Joy and I spent long hours at the crisis centre giving out food parcels and counselling people, and we didn't realise how we were going emotionally. We were falling apart and we didn't even know it; just living on adrenaline trying to get the town together and help the people … and the next thing we knew we no longer had a church. My wife was tired and just wanted some normality in her life.

Every minute we had available during the next six months we spent helping whoever we could to sort out their home, clean out the mud and restore their lives to some semblance of order. In the meantime, our own home remained in ruins and the cracks in our lives were widening.

The government had given everyone flood recovery money and six months after the flood we spent ours going to America. I had wanted to take the whole family to Pensacola for a long time, as well as visit friends we had made over the years, so when the opportunity arose (courtesy of the flood recovery money and some half-price fares) we took it.

The trip was wonderful, but after those eight weeks we came back to Katherine and reality hit us really hard. Somehow it was like we had been removed from the grieving process for that period of time but now we were right back where we started, right back at the state we were in immediately after the flood.

… the Katherine flood of 1998 changed everything—it washed us all away …

By the end of that year, Joy had left me. We had been together more than 22 years—since she was just 16. We had married the following year when she was 17 and raised a family together. She had been the greatest encourager in my life, telling me since I was first saved as a young man that God had a great plan for me. Joy spoke truth into me when all I knew was confusion and desperation.

> *"… the Katherine flood changed everything – it washed us all away …"*

All my life, since becoming a Christian at the age of 20, I had had prophecies and dreams. In 1994 when we first went to the Northern Territory, a pastor from New Zealand came to Katherine and said to me, "God has shown me that Katherine is only going to be for a time … God is going to send you out all around the world". At the time I had thought to myself, "How could I possibly go out from Katherine?". But Joy had constantly reminded me of that and the many other prophetic words that had been spoken over me.

She had stood by me while God dealt with my fractured and dysfunctional past and moulded me into His man … and now she was gone. She told me that she could no longer be my wife; that although she loved me she just couldn't do this anymore.

Ironically, on that same day, I had a phone call from Dr Josh Peters, who ran the missions program at Brownsville Revival Bible College, Pensacola. We had met the evangelist Steve Hill during our recent US trip and I had given my testimony while we were there. It had become quite a popular video. Funnily enough I think they viewed me as some kind of Crocodile Dundee! I was told that they wanted to send a team from Brownsville Revival Bible College to Katherine on a mission trip and Dr Peters asked if I would host them.

Everything in me wanted to say, "No, forget it! I can't do this! My whole life has just fallen apart …" But my spirit said otherwise and I found myself saying, "Yes. We can do that".

But the day my wife left was horrible, so horrible … I was left on my own in our old caravan with broken windows. I had hurt my back and could hardly walk because

The debris left behind after the water receded. You can see our piano in the front of the picture.

of the pain in my legs. The church we had worked so hard for was no longer ours; I was drowning in debt and now my wife had gone too.

Outside the caravan were big piles of our belongings, caked in mud. Out of the window I could see all the damage to the bottom floor of the house we had lived in for the past four years. There was nothing much left of our life except a pile of old boxes. One contained the cards we had given each other, and I sat there and read through the heartfelt promises that had now been broken: "I will love you forever … we will serve God together forever". I was absolutely devastated.

Soon after, the devil came to me and said, "You are finished. Your wife has left you and you will never preach again. You have lost everything, it is all gone".

I was so angry I stood up and yelled, "Well, I am going to serve God! I am going to serve God whatever it takes. I am not going to backslide or do anything stupid". I made a decision that I was going to keep following God and forgive those who had bitterly betrayed me, no matter what anyone else did. I had always told my children, "No matter what, don't get angry with God. He is a good God".

I could no longer preach in the church as naturally they felt I needed time to recover after the breakdown of our marriage, but I could still preach to the aboriginals. I began to spend more and more time in the outback. Nothing was going to stop me.

When the team from Brownsville came we had an amazing time, and saw phenomenal things happen. Before they left, the head of the team gave me some money and said to me, "We want you to come and speak on your missionary work to the Bible college students".

There I was, rejected by the church and by my wife, washed up and living in a broken down caravan, and I was being invited to speak at a Bible college that was born out of one of the most well-known moves of God in the last century! If that doesn't prove that God moves in mysterious ways I am not sure what does!

I struggled to forgive my wife for leaving me, but I had to. Eventually I chose to let go of the anger and bitterness before it could destroy me. I worked through the pain and the betrayal and let it go. It wasn't possible to hold on to my love for God and keep all of that burning in my heart.

The devastation also caused me to stop and think about myself and what part I had played in this tragic situation; to consider what I could have done differently. I had to take responsibility for my own failings and seek forgiveness.

I am not going to tell you this was a quick process. I couldn't even begin to describe how painful and heart-breaking this whole situation was. I am also not going to pretend that allowing God to heal me was easy or that I don't still have moments when my heart aches over what happened. The agony of losing your marriage is more extreme than any words can do justice to, but it is not my intention in this book to describe all the details. Instead I want to illustrate how this tragedy fuelled my hunger for God. In the end the only thing I wanted was more of Him because, to be brutally honest, He was the one who kept me alive.

While God didn't cause these tests and trials to happen, He did allow them and He did use them. Through what happened He built character in me and also made me aware of some of the attitudes and beliefs that I still needed to deal with.

Jesus said, "Many are called but few are chosen".[25] I

believe that between the calling and the choosing is the proving. Katherine was my proving ground. Dealing with the breakup of my marriage was all part of this. If I was to fulfil the call of God on my life, I had to have character strong enough to push through every trial and put God first in every part of my life.

God had given me a life and the most wonderful gift possible: the gift of salvation. Before I knew Him, I was tormented and without peace. How could I choose to turn away from Him? I felt so indebted for all He had done for me. There are times in life when we have to choose which path we will follow. It was as if I was standing at a crossroad and God was asking the question, "Will you still follow Me when everything you value has been stripped away?".

And the answer? I chose to follow my Lord wherever He would lead me.

When I see people suffering, an incredible compassion stirs in my heart and drives me to take action. I can't bear to see people in pain and do nothing, when I know that Jesus longs to heal them and set them free. All I wanted was to go where there were poor people and do what I could to help them.

Soon after, God began to speak to me about going to Mexico. I was all for it. With everything that had happened I certainly didn't want to stay in Katherine, and it seemed like Mexico was a place where I could make a difference.

CHAPTER THREE

The Outpouring Begins

Every day my relationship with God was growing stronger. I knew I needed Him desperately and prayer had always played a large part in my life, right from when I first became a Christian. When we had young children I had formed the habit of going for a long walk as this was the only way I could pray without distraction. At the time this was a means of escape but that habit would prove to be a great blessing. Every opportunity I had I would start talking to God, and I still do. As soon as I am not with people—even if that is just stepping out of the room to go to the bathroom—I start talking to Him. I am incredibly conscious of His presence with me all the time.

When God spoke to me about going to Mexico, I knew He would provide a way. Financially the situation looked impossible, but because of all the hard times we had been through where money was concerned, I had great faith to believe that He would somehow make it all happen.

When I announced to my family that I was going, my son Jamin immediately said, "Dad, I will go with you". Without hesitation he decided to leave the outback life to be by my side.

I was really pleased but it also meant two tickets had to be funded. However, through a string of God-ordained moments, Jamin and I were provided with tickets to fly to Mexico. The next big question was, "What would we do when we got there?".

I had absolutely nothing organised, nowhere to preach, nowhere to stay—nothing. But by faith we were going because I was sure that was what God wanted me to do.

A few weeks before we were to leave I was asked to speak in a church in Townsville about what Jamin and I would be doing in Mexico. Only I knew that nothing was in place but I also knew that God was in charge of the arrangements. He never does anything a minute too late! I got up in that pulpit and by faith told them how we were going to be travelling around to different churches, where I would preach salvation and pray for people saying, "… and there are people there right now just waiting to receive a miracle".

Ivan Nosworthy, the pastor of the COC church in Townsville, had been very kind to me and had encouraged us to go to Mexico. His church laid hands on us and prayed for us, asking God to bless us as we went.

About three days before we were due to fly out, I got an email asking me to preach in a church in Mexico. I have to admit that was a relief! It was the beginning of February 2000, and I wrote in my diary: *"Last day before leaving. It still hasn't quite hit us yet. There is a strong sense of destiny on us".*

Jamin and I flew to Los Angeles where Fred Keller, a local businessman, picked us up. Fred drove us to Yuma, Arizona, and a local pastor then took us to San Luis, just across the Mexican border. As I ministered in the church there, it dawned on me just how long it had been since I had preached from a church pulpit. The pastor's wife acted as my translator and it was a very powerful meeting.

The pastor and some of his colleagues later spoke to me and asked if I would speak at a men's night. He told me they were booked up after that so I would have to leave. When I shared my belief that God would do something [to keep us in Mexico] he just looked at me as if I was crazy!

The men's meeting went well and from there we went to Baja, California, where we spent about a week preaching and teaching every morning at a large children's home and orphanage called Rancho Santa Marta, which had been built within a Christian community. God really touched people's lives there and they asked me to come and be their resident pastor, however, I knew that wasn't in God's plan.

After that came Ensenada and one of the strangest

Jamin and I in the main street of San Luis with some local Mexican Indians.

experiences of our trip. The pastor at Ensenada didn't speak English and I didn't speak Spanish, so we couldn't really communicate. So that I could preach there, they recruited a local farm worker who didn't even believe in God, and he came to the meetings and interpreted for me. People were getting saved and healed from bad backs, depression and all kinds of things. When God revealed to me the demonic oppression in people's lives I boldly stated, "Come out in the name of Jesus". As this unsaved man repeated the words in Spanish the demons came out. The meetings were powerful, and afterwards I asked him if he would like to give his life to Jesus. I could hardly believe it when he said he wasn't interested!

Back in San Luis, we received a phone call asking us to go and pray for a church member's husband who had had a stroke. When we got to the hospital we were confronted with a terrible scene. The wife was crying as if her heart had broken and I couldn't begin to describe the fear in that man's eyes. He was only in his mid thirties, had a young family, and in a moment had gone from normality to being completely paralysed down one side of his body.

Jamin and I had been praying in our room for about an hour when we received the call to go to the hospital, so we were already stirred up to believe God for a miracle. We reached down and, laying our hands on the paralysed part of his body, began to pray and cry out to God for a miracle for this man. The pastor's wife had brought oil with her and we anointed his body as we prayed. After about an hour we were ready to leave and I turned to the pastor's wife and told her that I really believed God was working in his body, even though at that point we couldn't see anything and he couldn't feel any difference.

The next day was Sunday and during the church service we heard a big commotion behind us and people's voices crying out. Turning around in amazement, we saw the man we had been praying for just the previous night walk into the church without any assistance. You should have heard the people—they were so excited! As he walked up to me, he reached over and hugged me saying, "Gracias, gracias, gracias …". Hugging him back I quickly corrected him, "It wasn't us, it was God who touched you".

We found out later that after Jamin and I had left the hospital he began to receive the feeling and strength back into his body. His recovery was so rapid that they discharged him the following morning and he came straight to church.

Yolanda, a local business woman, arranged an itinerary

> *"… he had been paralysed but the next morning he walked into church as if nothing had happened!"*

and drove Jamin and I all over the country, giving me the opportunity to preach in many different churches. We saw a lot of really wonderful things. In fact, when we went into one city the power of God was so strong that even as people began to come forward for prayer they fell to the floor and were delivered without even being touched. It was awesome.

One morning I woke up to find that I was almost totally unable to speak. Most of the roads were dry and dusty, and the effect of breathing in all that dust, combined with some kind of virus, meant my voice was almost completely gone.

On that day I was scheduled to preach at three meetings in one church and then go across the border into America to preach at an evening service. I decided to lay hands on my throat and believe God for a miracle. But I still couldn't speak, other than just squeaking some whispers out.

I told Yolanda that I couldn't speak but was going to believe God. As I sat in the church waiting to be introduced nothing had changed, but as I stood up and walked to the pulpit the power of God suddenly came on me and I was able to preach. From nine o'clock in the morning to three o'clock in the afternoon, I spoke almost non-stop. Every time I stopped preaching my voice disappeared again.

Mexicans are not the best at keeping time and my anxiety about making it over the border in time for my next meeting was building. I kept saying, "We have to go, we have to go", feeling more and more concerned every minute. It didn't help that no-one there spoke English. Even Yolanda only knew a few words. When we finally got away I knew it was really late.

We arrived at the church an hour after the meeting had started to find that they were trying to keep the worship going, hoping that I would arrive any minute. I was exhausted and had no voice. It was insane, yet as I walked into the meeting the power of God came on me again and I was able to preach. God began to heal people. As soon as the meeting finished, my voice disappeared. It was the most amazing experience. When we got back to Yuma I went to stay at a friend's place, utterly exhausted.

Another time we went to a large city called Mexicali, on the US/Mexico border. We were in the worst area of the city, and people all around us were doing drugs and living in distress. We held a crusade in the middle of a big field, practically in the dark, and a large number of people turned up. My interpreter had spent 15 years in a Los Angeles prison for drugs and had been involved with gangs. He was a big man, covered in tattoos, and had learnt to speak English in prison. Halfway through my message he got so excited he started preaching without me! Then he began calling people up for prayer. He was so big I wasn't going to argue and he ended up virtually finishing my message for me. It was a funny experience but many people were touched by the miracle working power of God that night.

"... people all around us were doing drugs and living in distress."

We did quite a few meetings in Mexicali and they were very powerful. People were literally getting thrown to the ground under the power of God. By God's grace a lot of people were healed.

From Mexico we flew up to Pensacola, Florida, so that I could keep my commitment to Dr Josh Peters to speak at the Brownsville Bible College on missions. Many were healed but the miracle received by a young man who had been in a motorcycle accident stood out. He had badly damaged his leg and hip and could hardly walk. After prayer the pain left his leg and he was so excited he ran lap after lap around the huge auditorium screaming out, "Jesus, I'm healed, I'm healed, I'm healed!".

While we were still in Brownsville I received a letter from a pastor in Scotland, inviting me to come and speak at his church. Two and a half months before, when we were still in Australia, a church receptionist in Townsville had told me that she had just been to Scotland and mentioned, in passing, that she thought I should go there. Something about it struck a chord in my spirit and I had turned to Jamin at the time saying, "I think God wants us to go to Scotland". She gave us a list of six or seven churches and I sent them each a letter to let them know I was intending to visit.

No-one in Scotland had ever heard of me. In fact, no-one in Australia had either, and Crawford Kirkwood, the pastor of a small church in Wishaw, was the only one who responded. He told me that he had a church of just 12 people and could offer no financial support, but that if I would come he could arrange some meetings. Later on I found out that he had exaggerated. There were only 11 people and that included Crawford himself, his wife and daughter, a new baby, a little toddler, one guy who only came about once every three or four weeks because he kept getting angry with the pastor, and five other people.

I asked God what to do and felt strongly that Wishaw was where He wanted me to go despite the fact that Crawford's letter didn't exactly inspire me with any great hope! We planned to go to Scotland for a few weeks and then return to Mexico where I had been invited to minister at crusades and speak at conferences across the country.

Looking back now, I wonder if the church in Scotland was reaping what she had sown—some of my forebears had gone from Scotland to Australia and worked as missionaries to share the gospel in that new land. Now I was going to Scotland to do the same.

We flew to London from Brownsville and our first experience of Heathrow Airport was unbelievable. It was so busy and crowded, totally different to any place we had ever been. Having already booked into a youth hostel in the city, we headed for the train station. Not knowing where we were going, it was really confusing and the station was noisy and packed with people. While we were standing on the platform unsure of our next step, a train pulled up and the mass of people just surged towards the doors, taking Jamin with them. Before I knew it he had clambered aboard the train with his duffle bag and the doors had quickly shut behind him. I was left standing on the platform, holding all the money, both our passports and all our identification. Jamin was all alone, riding off into the sunset on a train. Neither of us even knew where it was going.

Panicked, I watched in disbelief as the train pulled out of the station, taking my son with it. When the next train arrived I made sure I got through those doors before they shut! I grabbed my bags and, pushing through the people, scrambled onto the train. We travelled through a couple of stations and I peered out every time, trying to see if Jamin was there. At the next stop, I caught sight of him and quickly called out as the doors opened. Amazingly, he heard me. I leapt out of the carriage and grabbed him in a big hug. We were laughing like crazy! Together this time, we caught the next train—still laughing like mad men. Neither of us could believe we had only been in London for a couple of hours and had managed to lose each other—and even more amazingly, find each other again in a city of more than seven million people—within that short space of time!

Unfortunately, this was only my first experience of loss

when travelling. I have since developed an uncanny ability to leave things all over the world!

After disembarking from the train, we started walking the last leg of our journey to the youth hostel. London's historic cobblestones were to prove a challenge. As I wheeled my heavy suitcase over those uneven streets the rough surface proved too much for it, and the wheels broke off, leaving me to drag it the rest of the way.

As you can imagine, it was a great relief when we finally arrived safely at the hostel and I was pleasantly surprised when we were shown to a dormitory room with no-one else in it. "Fantastic," I thought, "these youth hostels are pretty good really". Worn out by the excitement of our journey and a dose of jetlag, I tucked myself into a bottom bunk so I could more easily get in and out during the night, and in the quiet of the room went straight into a deep sleep.

Sometime later I felt this incredible pain in my face and cried out. A drunken voice slurred in response, "Sorry, mate", as its owner clambered over me. My face had been mistakenly used as a rung on the ladder used to get to the top bunk! I realised very quickly that the youth hostel was the crash pad for London's party animals and most occupants enter their rooms in the small hours of the morning.

Since that night I have always made sure I take the top bunk!

A few days later we left London and spent a week at a place near Newcastle, where we stayed with an Australian couple. During a visit to Ken Gott's church, I phoned Crawford and told him we would be arriving the following day. I don't think he had really expected to hear from me. He quickly arranged three meetings for the next Friday night, Saturday night and Sunday morning.

Wishaw is a small town on the west coast of Scotland not far from Glasgow and soon after our arrival I discovered that it is a town well known for its challenging social problems. Unemployment is still endemic and the rate of teenage pregnancies is one of the highest in Europe. It has been recorded that there are now fifth generation welfare recipients living there. Children who have never seen either their father or grandfather work are reasonably common.

Substance abuse and violence are part of everyday life there and many Scots refuse to drive through the town—even though it takes much longer to go around it—because of their fear.

These problems have been exacerbated by the long-standing bigotry between the Catholics and Protestants. The population is separated into these two very distinct groups. The Protestants are known as the "Covenanters", and hold demonstrations and marches against the Catholics. The Catholics have the same antipathy towards the Protestants. Near Crawford's church there are two schools side by side—one Catholic, one Protestant. In town there are two pubs—one Catholic, one Protestant.

When we first arrived, I was warned not to wear a blue shirt and black pants, as that is the uniform of the Catholics and could have resulted in my becoming a target for Protestant violence.

Crawford and his wife Sheila had valiantly given up an executive lifestyle in a nice suburb to live in run-down tenement housing in Wishaw. Their goal was to reach "the worst of the worst" and they chose to live amongst them. In doing so they had been attacked and abused and had two cars torched, amongst other things.

It was there, in "Coltness Estate", that Jamin and I would live while we were in Wishaw. As we walked into the building, the smell of sour urine was almost overpowering on the tenement stairs and signs of dried vomit were obvious. At night the music from the drunken, drug-filled parties was so loud it was almost impossible to think.

Since we had arrived in Wishaw on a Monday, Jamin and I were free of commitments until the following Friday when Crawford had been able to arrange, at the last minute, for us to hold a meeting in a local hall. As soon as we settled in we began to walk around the streets and pray, calling upon the power of God. I tried to talk to people in the township and they didn't even bother to respond. They were so unfriendly it wasn't even possible to get a conversation started, which is not something I usually find difficult!

The church owns a second-hand shop in the main street that is run as both an outreach to the local people and a way of raising money. When I went inside the shop to try to connect with the people I didn't get anywhere.

It was so frustrating that I walked the streets crying out to God, "Father please touch these people". Crawford had told me that for the previous four years there hadn't been one soul saved. There was such an incredible heaviness over the place, such hatred between the Catholics and the Protestants. Such bigotry, such massive social problems. But often that is so like the Lord; in the worst environments, His love, mercy and amazing grace shine all the more brightly.

The hall that had been hired for the Friday night meeting was in a nearby village called Craig Neuk. At that time, Craig Neuk was considered to be the worst of the worst, with more problems and social issues than Wishaw. Even the police wouldn't venture in there because of the crime and the violence. On top of that, the hall was actually in two sections and when we arrived there we found out there was a spiritualist meeting going on in one side while our meeting was on in the other. Consequently we had the most challenging meeting you could ever imagine. Only 15 people turned up, including my son and I, a few visitors and most of the congregation of the church.

That night one young lady recommitted her life to Christ, and a woman who had battled with alcohol received salvation, which was wonderful. However, it didn't seem that there was anything else significant going on here at all. Being used by now to seeing God move more powerfully than this, I went home feeling pretty disheartened. All I could think was, "Have I come all this way for just 15 people?". Really only 13 if you took Jamin and me out of the count!

Pastor Crawford Kirkwood introduces me to the "crowd" at the second meeting in Wishaw.

Crawford was also quite depressed. We had all been hoping for something more.

However, something changed the very next morning when I went with Crawford to a men's breakfast where a preacher called Tommy Baird was sharing. I found him difficult to understand because of his broad Scottish accent, but when he began talking about souls and hungering for revival, I was stirred. Praying and crying out to God I felt something happen. I could sense in my spirit that today was the day. I just knew we were going to see God move.

When we left the men's breakfast I walked into the second-hand store and "just like that" a door opened and I began to talk to a lady and share about the Lord. I laid hands on her and began to pray and she gave her life to Jesus.

About 15 minutes later a notorious alcoholic walked in off the street. I told him about the love of God and he too gave his life to Christ. I laid hands on him and as the power of God touched him he rolled on the floor and was delivered from his addiction. Two people had been saved in a period of about 20 minutes. Shortly afterwards another person gave their life to Christ. It was amazing.

That night when we began the meeting, 23 people turned up and five people gave their lives to the Lord.

In the space of one day eight people had made decisions for Christ in this place where the spiritual landscape had been dry and dusty for years.

Something had broken in the spirit world over Wishaw. I could feel it. That night I prayed for a woman called Barbara Downie and God gave her the most phenomenal creative miracle. At the age of five a pencil had been forced into her ear, which destroyed the delicate internal mechanism and left her with a totally ruined eardrum. This was a terribly painful condition and for the past 50 years she had not been able to travel in an aeroplane, drive or go swimming. All her life she had been on a pension.

I prayed for Barbara several times before the meeting but all that happened was her pain actually increased. But that night I laid hands on her and the power of God touched her. I put my hand over the ear that was damaged and she fell to the ground and lay there for about an hour. Then she began to laugh uncontrollably. In fact, she couldn't walk and had to be carried out of the meeting. We had no idea at that stage what had happened, other than that she had obviously had a fairly significant encounter with God.

A number of other people got healed from painful conditions. One was a little baby who had been almost completely covered in eczema. Following the meeting the child's mother called Crawford to tell him that the child's skin was totally clear.

We were incredibly excited. It was like a corner had been turned, like destiny … something was breaking through, something was happening over Wishaw. God was healing people.

The next morning we were ready to start the Sunday service when I heard a woman's voice screaming and squealing. Barbara Downie came in, laughing, spinning around and just bubbling over with joy, saying, "I am healed, I am healed!"

She shared with us about her condition, which had been so bad that she had to be connected to a machine every night. The machine would wake her husband if she had a fit so he could make sure she didn't swallow her tongue. He would then have to settle her down and give her medication if she needed it. Barbara's husband was on a part carer's pension to look after her because the situation was so intense.

Barbara also lacked balance, which often caused her to fall over. Sometimes if the wind was too strong she would fall over in the street because her balance couldn't adjust. It took her about an hour to get up every morning because she couldn't get orientated.

Continuing to squeal with excitement, Barbara said, "This morning I got up and I had no pain. I slept beautifully and I didn't have any fits. For the first time in 50 years my balance is perfect!". It was absolutely incredible.

> *"In a matter of minutes, God had given Barbara a brand new eardrum …"*

That same day she contacted a friend of hers who was a specialist at the hospital in the Emergency Ward and told him what had happened. When he came to see her he got out his stethoscope and his mirror to examine her ear and said, "Barbara, I can't believe this". He knew her case well and with amazement he told her, "I can see a brand new shiny eardrum in there—you have a new eardrum!". She had not had a functioning eardrum for 50 years.

From there she went back to her GP and he examined her and sent her to a neurosurgeon. She went to another doctor. They did scans on her head and couldn't believe the results. She had had seven major operations on her head that had caused severe internal scarring (all of which had failed) and the doctor said there was no sign of any of them. Five years later, when I last saw her, she was still perfect. Barbara ended up getting her license, she got a clean bill of health to fly on a plane, to swim, to do all the things she never dreamed she would be able to. She has also been able to get a job and stop being dependent on the pension, which was something that was never going to be possible before God stepped in.

It was this creative miracle that sparked an incredible awakening in Scotland, a brand new thing.

Encouraged by what had happened, Crawford asked me if I would stay the following weekend and hold another meeting. It was a step of faith for both of us and I agreed to stay.

Meanwhile other invitations came through him from pastors in different regions in Scotland, so I spent the week

A smiling Barbara Downey is shown here working on signs to advertise the healing meetings in Wishaw, while Sheila Kirkwood takes phone enquiries.

travelling around and ministering in various towns before returning to Wishaw the following Friday. That night about 30 or 40 people turned up and there were more healings and miracles. Crawford asked if I could stay another week and once again I agreed. That week about 50 or 60 people turned up, and more people's lives were changed.

Jamin and I walked all over town praying for God to move. I began to speak to the people, stepping up to shop counters to tell the attendants about Christ. If I saw someone in a shop who was sick I laid hands on that person and shared the gospel with them. During those first few weeks, we saw about 50 people give their lives to Jesus. After four years of drought it was like a revival.

About the third time Crawford asked me to stay another week I knew the time had come to make a decision. Would I stay in Scotland or return to Mexico as I had said I would, to do a national tour? After seeking God for an answer, I received two different prophecies from two men of God I knew back in Australia, both telling me to stay. Although it was a difficult decision, I knew in my spirit it was what God wanted. For that time, Scotland was where we were supposed to be.

In those first weeks, Jamin and I often went out on to the streets. Once we stood at the traffic lights in downtown Wishaw and when the cars stopped I began to preach about the love and grace of God. We publicly worshipped Jesus to the sounds of Jamin's guitar and the hum of the surrounding traffic.

I got some posters printed and spread them around town. Like a traffic sign they boldly proclaimed, "STOP! Do you need a miracle? Come and receive a miracle at Wishaw this Friday night". As soon as the vandals tore them down we went out and put them up again.

One day I was down on the main street with a group of new Christians that I was training up in evangelism and street ministry. Usually we just handed out tracts and shared the gospel. But this time I put my Bible on the pavement and covered it with my coat before yelling out, "Be careful, stand back!" and acting as if the lump under my coat was caused by something really dangerous. Soon a crowd of people were standing around and I cried out, "Be careful, its alive, its alive!". I moved forward as if I was trying to catch this dangerous thing that had been let loose and everyone was trying to work out what was going on. As soon as I had their attention I rushed out, pulled my jacket back, grabbed my Bible and begin to preach John 3:16, *"… for God so loved the world"*. At other times I stood up on a statue in town with my Bible calling out to the people to give their lives to Jesus Christ.

There were people who came to the meetings and gave their lives to the Lord and some who got healed, just from us being out on the streets, even though a lot of people thought we were crazy.

I also began to train up a music team. We had started with just Jamin playing guitar, but then God brought two young girls along, Natalie and Lynne, who are both very passionate for God and have beautiful singing voices. Another musician called Derek also travelled with us, as did Natalie's brother Adam whenever he could. No matter where we were, if I felt the time was right I asked them to start worshipping. We saw God move on planes, in trains, wherever we went. Whenever we started praising God His presence would come like a flood.

All of this sparked quite a bit of attention and more pastors and ministers began to contact me and invite me to their churches to share what was happening. The word started to spread that something phenomenal was happening at Wishaw.

After about five or six weeks I got too busy to go out on the streets in Wishaw and I began to do outreaches all around Scotland and in some areas of England. They were exciting days! I often say that God just set me up—I had never expected to see something like this happen. God opened all the doors, God moved the people, God did the miracles and the whole thing has just gone from there to this day.

It took me a while to adjust to what was happening. Coming from the Northern Territory and then Mexico and seeing the power of God move with the passionate indigenous people was really different from seeing it happen in this incredibly oppressed area of Scotland, populated by the normally staunch Scots. Many of us have heard of amazing miracles happening in Latin countries, where the people purportedly have more "faith", but here was God moving, just as powerfully, in a place where it had almost seemed faith was dead.

The many healings and salvations caught the attention of the church and the nation. One of the testimonies reported in the newspapers[26] was the story of Margaret Neely, from Northern Ireland. I love to tell this story. The Bible is full of stories about women with great faith, but Margaret is a modern woman of faith and how God moved in her life is truly remarkable.

Our paths first crossed after a friend of Margaret's

invited her to a meeting we were holding in Lanark, Scotland, and told her about all the incredible miracles that had been happening.

Margaret had been crippled for nine and a half years after a serious assault left her with a spinal injury. Shortly after being attacked, she caught tuberculosis, which damaged her internal organs and left her in chronic pain. For the first four or five years of her illness Margaret was severely depressed. Her self-esteem and confidence had ebbed away and she was often suicidal. During that time she could only lay on her couch or on her bed, crippled with pain. It took five years before she graduated to a wheelchair.

In more recent years her health had deteriorated very quickly and carers had to come in each day to dress her and take care of her personal needs. For the five months prior to

---

Is Wishaw new pilgrim place?

Michelle Gallagher reports

Do you believe in miracles, that Jesus raised the dead and turned water into wine? ... We live in an age where people seem to put more trust in science than God, so it's hardly surprising people find it impossible to believe anything other than science in the form of modern medicine will save them when they're ill. [But] suddenly a lot of people in Wishaw aren't sure ...

He [John] said: "Since I got here a little girl has been cured of autism, a woman has joints in her toes where there were none, cancerous tumours have disappeared and people suffering from MS and arthritis have been cured. People often are afraid or very sceptical, but once they see the miracles they know this isn't a con.

Excerpt from article published in the Wishaw Press.

---

our meeting, her whole body had been shutting down. The doctors had done tests but told her she was so severely disabled they could do nothing for her. Her body was dying.

In response to the stories her friend had told her of how God was moving, she came to a meeting in Lanark. There were renovations going on downstairs which meant we could only hold meetings on the second floor so she was carried up the stairs in her wheelchair before being wheeled up the front.

God was doing miracles everywhere, but when I prayed for Margaret, nothing happened. I came back and prayed for her probably four or five times but still nothing happened. She sat slumped in her wheelchair and her face looked devoid of hope.

I bent down and quietly spoke these words in her ear, "Don't you give up, you come again and I will pray for you again".

A week or two later, Margaret came back to the same place. Once again, four men carried her upstairs in her wheelchair. I prayed for her several times and once again nothing happened.

Again I encouraged her, "Don't give up believing God for a miracle. I have seen miracles before. I have seen the crippled walk".

Margaret went back to Ireland and then came back again a third time. The four men carried her up again, I prayed for her again and still nothing happened.

But this time, when she went back to Belfast, she began to feel a weird sensation in her body. Strangely enough, the pain increased, but she also began to feel strength slowly coming back into her body. Something was happening, yet she was still crippled. Afterwards she told me that she was even able to stand out of her chair, just for a moment at a time.

The changes that were happening in her body encouraged her to come back a fourth time. On this occasion, I was preaching at Wishaw and when Margaret came through the door of the church I said to her, "Tonight, God is going to heal you and you are going to walk!".

She thought I was crazy.

I still remember how a moment came while I was preaching when I just knew the time was NOW! I called out to the congregation, "Someone here is going to receive a miracle tonight!". Just about everyone there, including Margaret, started looking left and right, trying to work out who it was going to be. I pointed straight at her and said, "The miracle is for you!".

At this stage she was sitting about two-thirds of the way towards the back of the congregation. I walked up to her with a smile on my face because I knew what God was going to do. I prayed and then, taking her by the hand, pulled her up saying, "Stand up and walk".

And she did.

As she began to walk she also started to cry. Then she started to laugh, then she cried some more, she laughed and she cried and she walked all at the same time!

Within an hour after she arrived home that night, Margaret's internal organs also started to work properly for the first time in nine and a half long years. Every day she did something new. Her doctor was totally shocked but overjoyed when she walked into his surgery.

Margaret belonged to a Presbyterian church and when she rang her minister and said, "I'm healed, I'm healed," no-one could believe it until she walked into the church and told them what Jesus had done. Two weeks later, she was captured on video dancing in church.

Five years later, Margaret returned from her second mission trip to Africa. She can even run.

The word had spread and when we went to Peterhead for five nights of meetings, they had to change venues because so many people turned up. In the end, they hired the ballroom of the largest hotel in town for the final two nights. We saw many salvations and re-dedications to the Lord and many expressed a new fire in their faith in Christ. There was an incredibly strong presence of the Holy Spirit and it was not uncommon for people to be literally thrown to the floor when they were prayed for.

"Margaret's body was shutting down and she was dying ... five years later she returned from her second missionary trip to Africa!"

On one of those last two nights, I was in the hall about an hour before the meeting. The worship band was practising and even at that early time, people were trickling in for the meeting. While I was sitting there, I noticed a lady come hobbling into the meeting on a walking stick. She was obviously struggling.

Feeling compassion for her obvious pain, I walked up to her before the meeting even started. This lady's name was Beth and she was from the local Baptist church. Beth told me that she suffered from lupus[27] and arthritis. Her body was wracked with pain and her legs no longer functioned properly. I told Beth that God could heal her right then and there and she agreed that I could pray for her.

When I put my hand on her head and prayed the power of God flowed through her like electricity and she fell to the floor. I stood her up and she fell to the floor. I tried again and she fell to the floor again. She was shaking when she finally got to her feet. Taking her stick from her, I just simply said, "walk!".

The auditorium we were in was pretty large and Beth started walking around and around and around, crying the whole time. For years she had suffered terrible pain and that night God healed her.

Beth was fairly well known in Peterhead and everyone was amazed when she walked out the front at the start of the meeting and testified how she had just been waiting for the meeting to start when Jesus set her free.

She could hardly open her hands when she came in, and couldn't lift her arms at all, but that all changed when Jesus touched her life and she was totally healed. I wish you could have seen her face.

When she presented herself to her therapist she needed no treatment and the therapist wept in amazement. Beth's phone rang hot all day. It caused quite a stir amongst the Baptists since, as she joyfully pointed out, "John, you must understand that as Baptists we don't believe in healing … but I do now!". Beth attended the rest of the meetings in Peterhead to share her testimony, so overcome by the miracle God had done.

After hearing this wonderful story, a man from the Methodist church who hadn't worked for six years because of severe injuries to his knees came out for prayer. He told me he had only come to the meeting to "have a look" but his knees were absolutely wrecked and he was in terrible pain. I just placed my hands on his knees and then told him to move them. When he realised he no longer had any pain he couldn't believe it and he began jumping up and down like a wild man. Later, he wrote a testimony of how he had suffered for years and God had healed him. He was so completely restored he even took up jogging!

The next night the Methodist minister and his eldership turned up and sat right at the back. They knew the pain that man had been in and were curious as to how this miracle had happened. I eventually laid hands on the minister who fell down under the power of the Holy Spirit. The eldership followed suit after similar prayer.

It was during these meetings that a young girl called Nicola who suffered from autism improved dramatically after prayer. The next day when she went to her special school the teachers wept in unbelief. Her mother, Elizabeth, who had adopted her as an orphan from Romania, couldn't believe it. When a visiting psychologist examined the child the previous diagnosis was questioned because there was no longer any evidence of autism. Her coordination was restored and her leaking bowel had been healed. She had been deaf in one ear but could now hear. Her mother just kept hugging this beautiful little girl and weeping as she testified. The girl had not spoken until that night and she kept calling out, "Hallelujah! God is so good!". Months later Elizabeth testified that her daughter was amazing her teachers by her phenomenal progress and was now bringing homework home from school.

I could write pages on the healings—on pain leaving bodies, addicts being relieved from addictive symptoms, depression leaving minds and many conditions disappearing. However, the greatest miracles were the shining joyful faces of those who came into relationship with Christ and those who rediscovered the joy of really knowing Him. What a privilege to serve Him!

Another fantastic thing about Peterhead was that people were queuing up to get into church more than an hour

This is a picture of Nicola in my arms. She was so profoundly changed after prayer that a psychologist questioned her previous diagnosis.

before the meetings were due to start. This was unheard of!

One man had been a schizophrenic for 30 years and when I prayed for him he screamed and collapsed on the floor. He came to the rest of the meetings that week and testified that he was off medication and no longer hearing voices. His wife of 14 years shared that she had never seen her husband so happy or behaving so normally. When his psychiatrist examined him, he was amazed by the man's behaviour and couldn't explain why all of a sudden he was so happy.

Another man arrived in great pain because of several cracked vertebrae in his spine. When I prayed for him the pain left instantly. The look of disbelief on his face when he realised all the pain had disappeared was priceless.

Towards the end of August I spoke at a leadership impartation meeting. It was my twentieth meeting in 22 days. That is not including day meetings, home visitations to pray for the sick, counselling sessions, meeting with pastors and leaders and travel time!

When we went to Aberdeen, an influential city of 250,000 people, they held a three-day city-wide crusade. All the churches came together to organise it and they were very excited, to say the least. The church leadership was believing God for revival to hit their city and when we returned a month or so later, the churches had grown considerably because of all the people who had come into relationship with God. One pastor told me he was going to have to knock down a wall to make enough room in his church!

When we returned to Lanark to hold some more meetings, I prayed for a woman who had suffered from severe depression for many years. After prayer she spent most of the service laughing and smiling and rolling on the carpet. A psychiatrist who knew her testified at the end of the week of the dramatic change in her life and behaviour. For the previous week, instead of lying in bed with black depression bombed out on medication she was cheerfully arising early and happily going about her daily life. She testified of her wonderful, newfound joy in the Lord.

One night in Wishaw I prayed for a girl who was cross-eyed and as I prayed her eyes straightened up! I was really excited, as were the people around us. When I looked around at them, I noticed a lady struggle out of her seat and begin shuffling towards the back of the building, leaning heavily on her walking frame and obviously intending to leave. I cried out to her, "Where do you think you are going? Don't you know the rules? No walking sticks are allowed outside the building!".

> *"Don't you know the rules? No walking sticks are allowed outside the building!"*

As the lady looked at me in shock (the rest of the congregation did too as you can imagine), I walked up to her and asked why she hadn't come down for prayer. "I was too scared", she told me. "I have arthritic knees and people were falling over. I am afraid that if I fell over I would never be able to get back up again."

I pulled out a plastic chair for her to sit on and encouraged her that God could heal her right then and there. Praying, I laid my hands on her knees and all of a sudden the power of God hit her like electricity and she went stiff as a board. She went so stiff in that flimsy plastic chair she almost broke the back of it! A moment later she just jumped up and ran down the aisle as fast as she could, like a charging rhino. She ran right down the middle and right back and then started leaping and dancing around the church. God had totally healed her knees. She walked out of the meeting that night carrying her stick in her hands with great joy. The friends who had brought her couldn't believe it! God is so good!

After that, this wonderful lady travelled many times to various meetings to give her testimony, and I would introduce her to the congregation as "the one who almost got away". On one memorable occasion, I couldn't believe it when, as she was in the middle of sharing her testimony and telling the story of how she had nearly left the building without receiving her miracle, I saw a lady stand up and start shuffling towards the back door leaning on her walking stick.

"Where do you think you're going?" I yelled brashly.

Much to my dismay, she replied in a frail voice, "I'm going to the toilet, dear". The whole meeting erupted into laughter and I have been too embarrassed to ask that question ever since!

With all that was going on, I had no doubt that God wanted to get the attention of the Scottish nation. While God was moving in this way wherever we went around the country, the meetings at Wishaw also kept growing and it wasn't long before the hall was packed and people were coming from everywhere. Doctors brought their patients and gave their lives to Jesus after seeing the incredible works

He was doing. As word spread people began to travel from England and even France, then South Africa and America. Some even came from Australia after finding out about it on the internet.

When the newspapers began to do stories about the miracles even more people came. It was like an Australian bushfire. Once it started to burn there was nothing that was going to stop it. All it had taken was a spark to catch alight.

Not everyone who experienced the power and presence of God remained grateful for it, however. One night I prayed for a lady who had been crippled and in a wheelchair for many years due to severe arthritis. When I prayed for her, God straightened her bones. She got out of her wheelchair and was dancing and twirling all around the church. The pastor was really shaken by it because she had been in a wheelchair for so many years. She no longer had any pain and was walking around the congregation shaking hands and receiving congratulations on her miracle. People were hugging her and celebrating with her because they were so happy that she had been set free in this way.

"It was like an Australian bushfire. Once it started to burn there was nothing that was going to stop it."

On the trip home, the friend driving her was sharing her excitement at being healed and said something along the lines of, "It is so good you are healed now! You will be able to get a job and you won't have to get government support to subsidise your phone, electricity and rent ...".

Suddenly the woman went completely quiet. When they got to her house, her friend took her wheelchair, which she no longer needed, out of the car and into the house. They walked through the front door and the woman turned her wheelchair around and sat back in it. She had realised that to her, it was much more comfortable being sick. All the pain came back on her again and she lost her healing.

Sometimes, no matter what God does, people don't really want to be healed.

CHAPTER FOUR

The Fire Spreads

Invitations were coming from Ireland and remote villages in the Scottish Isles, like Lewis and Harris, as well as France, Germany and Spain and I began to travel everywhere I could. I was so keen I was crazy, often preaching six or seven days a week. Sometimes I went for two weeks without a break, preaching every day in addition to visiting hospitals or different people in their homes and praying for God to grant healings or miracles. It was an incredibly exciting time.

After a few weeks I told Crawford that I would give him every single Friday night as well as a whole week of crusades every six weeks or so. I had originally gone to Wishaw to speak at three meetings, to be held over a single weekend. I ended up staying eight months!

No matter what happened, I always kept my promise to be in Wishaw on Friday night, even if it meant travelling from some remote area of Scotland, in the Highlands, or on one of the islands. There was one occasion when I was in France and in order to reach Wishaw to preach that Friday night I had to catch a taxi at four in the morning to get to the train station. Then I caught a train to Barcelona (Spain), before changing to an airport train. I flew to London and waited for a plane to Glasgow, where someone picked me up and drove me post-haste to Wishaw. I arrived just as they announced me to preach!

There is no doubt we had some close shaves, but no matter what, every Friday night during those eight months, I preached at Wishaw and God did outstanding miracles. There were blind eyes opened, deaf ears were able to hear again, the crippled walked and previously dumb voices were lifted up in gratitude to God.

One night an elderly lady of about 70 years of age was practically carried into the meeting by her daughter and granddaughter and laid in one of the rows of seats towards the front. Her legs were crippled and her hands had been locked into fists for about seven or eight years. That night I preached about the power of Jesus; the power of His blood, and how God not only forgives but He also heals and delivers. When I called people forward for prayer, this lady was carried out to give her life to Jesus. As I stepped up to her, I said, "Jesus has got a miracle for you".

As I laid hands on her the power of God flowed through those weak limbs and I told her family to lower her onto her legs. They manoeuvred her so that she was standing but they were taking her weight. Her family were amazed when they saw that she could stand up. I took her by the hands, saying, "walk".

I held her hands, and with her daughter and granddaughter crying uncontrollably nearby, this woman walked for the first time in many years. When I let her go she began to walk up and down the church on her own. As I prayed for her again the power of God touched her and she fell to the floor.

Although she could now walk, her hands, ruined by the arthritis she had suffered from for years, were still clenched tightly into fists, so her daughter brought them to my attention.

Then something happened that I will never forget. I reached out and gently touched each hand with my finger saying, "Open in the name of Jesus". Before my eyes both hands slowly unfurled, just like a rose bud or a flower opening its petals up to the sun. They kept opening until they were completely normal.

Shortly afterwards, in a very rare quiet moment, I was thinking about everything that had happened and wondering what on earth was going on. How could these people receive such incredible healings when I prayed for them? Me. John Mellor.

> *"Before my eyes both of her hands slowly unfurled ..."*

It was amazing that I had even made it through life this far, let alone become an evangelist and travelled to the other side of the world to pray for people. While I was contemplating this, Jesus showed me a vision. With my spirit I could see myself standing at the altar, placing my hands on this woman and asking God to heal her. I saw Jesus standing with me, and as I placed my hands on her, He placed His hands on mine and released His power. Once again I saw her hands opening up before me like beautiful rosebuds unfurling and my eyes filled with tears.

During this time I had the incredible privilege of meeting Derek Prince, an internationally recognised Bible teacher who has since gone to be with the Lord. Derek was amazed when he heard of the miracles that had been happening in Scotland. We spoke about the spiritual issues there and he said it was the darkest place he had ever been in. Derek also consoled and encouraged me about the painful break-up of my marriage, which I really appreciated.

The spiritualist church is very strong in Scotland and this country is also the home of Freemasonry. There are many "faith healers"[28] and witchcraft is incredibly prevalent. Thousands of standing stones where the ancient druids performed their sacrifices litter the landscape, as do druid graves and ceremonial grounds, especially in the north.

In a nation of 5,000,000, I preached in the biggest churches and yet these congregations were no larger than about 400 people. For some reason the church had never really grown. The suffering the Scots have experienced at the hands of the English has resulted in a deep resentment for many people. All these factors combined to create a place where there were deep spiritual strongholds.

Nevertheless, the invitations continued. We saw more healings and miracles, and the major Scottish newspapers published stories[29]. The newspapers even contacted the powers that be in the medical world, and asked how these miracles could be happening. It was no great surprise to us that they didn't have any answers!

The whole thing was so incredible it was surreal, almost as if it wasn't really happening. I prayed for people in public, at bus stations, in train stations, on aeroplanes, and saw people get healed out on the streets.

A lady came into the second-hand shop in Wishaw and asked me to pray over a handkerchief belonging to a friend who was scheduled to have surgery for a brain tumour. The doctors had given her only a few months to live and were operating in a last desperate attempt to save her life. After the hanky was laid on this lady she felt better and when they examined her prior to surgery, the tumour had completely disappeared. God is so amazing!

While travelling to different cities and even countries to minister to people was very satisfying, seeing God move in smaller gatherings was just as amazing. This was particularly true when I came across a woman called Linda Mason who lived in the village of Carluke, not too far from Wishaw.

Linda had been suffering from ME[30] for four years, and it had left her so tired and crippled that she couldn't even cook for her two children. I remember her telling me that all she could do was get up and throw some things in the microwave very quickly. Shopping was very difficult, especially standing in line at the checkout, and she would spend hours of every day in bed.

Although she had been a successful medical practitioner, Linda had been so adversely affected by her illness that she could no longer work.

A friend told Linda that someone was going to be holding a Bible study in Carluke and she decided to come along. While she had a faith in God, Linda didn't know that He still heals today.

Her friend encouraged her to come forward for prayer. As I laid hands on her the power of God touched her and she fell to the floor of the living room. It was something she was definitely not expecting. I asked God for His healing power to deliver her and set her free, and shortly afterwards the other people there helped her up and someone drove her home.

Something amazing had happened during that brief meeting. When Linda woke up the next morning she felt as if all the strength had returned to her body. In fact, she felt so good, she later told me, it was as if she was jumping out of her skin. Linda's energy levels were so strong she went out for a long walk, and then a jog. Her neighbours couldn't believe it when they saw her jogging. The following day she went to the pool and swam 24 laps. A few days later she climbed a hill. It had been four long and painful years since she could do anything like that.

The power of God had instantly delivered her and she was able to return to medical practice. Linda has since returned to Nepal (where she previously worked) for short mission trips and also goes mountain climbing!

Sometime afterwards, Linda and another doctor, Liz Doherty, brought a terminally ill patient to one of our meetings in Wishaw. This man had just a short time left to live. After pulling up in the car outside the hall, these two wonderful women of faith came in to see me. They told me that their patient was very seriously ill and close to death. Cancer had taken over one side of his lung, travelling throughout his body and down one arm. The pain was so extreme he had to be given morphine. Linda and Liz had brought him to the meeting because without a miracle, there was no hope for him. They had already seen what God could do and knew a miracle was possible.

Because he was suffering so much, they asked me to pray for him quickly. He couldn't cope with staying too long so I told them that if they brought him into the meeting, I would make sure that he was the first person I prayed for as soon as I finished preaching.

During my sermon, the moment came when I knew God was telling me to pray for him. They helped him forward and sat him in a chair out the front. I laid my hands on his head and began to pray, "In the name of Jesus, I take authority over this cancer". Putting my hand over the area of his lung, and then his cancerous arm, I continued to boldly pray.

When I asked him how he felt, his facial expression was almost frozen in shock as he told me the terrible pain he had been suffering appeared to be gone. "Well, stand up then," I said, and this man, who had struggled in with someone on either side to help him, stood straight up on his own just like a soldier. He even amazed himself!

"His facial expression was almost frozen in shock; the terrible pain was gone."

Incredibly, there was no longer any pain in his body and he started walking up and down the front of the church normally.

I told the musicians to strike up a tune, and asked one of the ladies, Mrs Sampson, to dance with him. Joyfully, they began to waltz. The people were cheering and clapping because they could see how ill this man had been and how the power of God had touched him. I asked the musicians to speed the music up and next thing they were jiving to rock and roll. This man, who moments before had been on the edge of death, swung Mrs Sampson around as if he was an

18-year-old boy. He was totally healed. Yet the greatest miracle was this: before he left that building, he gave his life to Jesus Christ. He recognised the power and majesty of God and walked out of that place a completely different man.

When we returned to hold some meetings in Aberdeen, some local church leaders commented to us about how the spiritual atmosphere had changed for the better since we had been there four weeks before. Aberdeen has been called a church graveyard, because apparently more churches have closed down there than any other known city in Europe. Churches once stood on every corner but now they have been converted into pubs, nightclubs and restaurants. Men of God had been praying for a revival in the city for some time.

> *"One of the most exciting transformations involved a man who had been a Satanist for 10 years."*

During the meetings, a number of people testified of having being miraculously healed and many were saved. One of the most exciting transformations involved a man who had spent many years in prison and had been a Satanist for 10 years. After prayer, he was delivered and laughed and cried for two days. He testified that it was the first time he had ever experienced love in his life; those who knew him couldn't believe the transformation.

The flood of miracles was impossible to keep up with and testimonies kept pouring in from all over the country. It got to the point where I couldn't relate in words all that God was doing—I still find it difficult. This is such a small fraction of all that went on and I just couldn't keep up with it all.

One morning at a meeting in Grove, an ex-boxer from New Zealand came forward to give his life to Jesus and as I prayed for him, suddenly fell backwards. When he got off the floor he asked me, "Did you hit me?" He told me that he had felt someone hit him. God had laid him out!

At another meeting in Grove, four people tried to leave and I ran out of the church and confronted them with the gospel. Everyone in the meeting was looking around, wondering what was going on. The music team didn't know what to do—no-one did. I don't think they had ever experienced the preacher running out of a meeting before! But the confusion was well worth it. All four people gave their lives to the Lord and one ended up on the hallway floor and was set free from the anxiety disorder known as agoraphobia. These

> "... the distinctive sound of the machine guns could be heard ..."

people had never experienced the power of God before.

In Northern Ireland we ministered in a church that had been burned down twice and has known terrible persecution because of all the political strife in that land. Nineteen years earlier the church had been violently attacked by the IRA. Men with balaclavas stood outside during a service, raking the wooden walls of the building with their machine guns firing, spraying the people inside with bullets. They then walked to the back of the building and stood at the door, shooting those inside. Tragically, three people were killed and about 14 were wounded.

When I visited there were still many people in the church who had been there that night. The pastor told me they were singing "Power in the Blood" when it happened. The service was being recorded and the distinctive noise of the machine guns could be heard when the tape was played back. These incredible people showed me the bullet holes still evident in the timber walls. The pastor's wife had injured her arm in the attack and had been suffering from it ever since. Praise God that after prayer she was completely healed.

On the train going to Aberdeen for a meeting, I noticed a group of women drinking and partying. I started to quietly pray for them and when they got off the train God gave me an opportunity to talk to them about all the miracles that had been happening and of His love for them. One of the ladies told me that she had a condition similar to lupus and was in great pain in the joints of her knees and elbows. I assured her that Jesus could heal that condition and offered to pray for her. She readily agreed even though we were in the public walkway. As I prayed the power of the Lord hit her and she began to cry uncontrollably. She then exclaimed that she felt "heat" in the joints of her body. Realising that all the pain had disappeared, she began to bend her legs and move her arms up and down. The lady and all her friends were totally amazed. I was just about to lead her in prayer to receive the Lord when her daughter cried out for her to come. The opportunity was lost for salvation but I have no doubt God will finish what He started that day, if He hasn't already. The Lord wants us to reach out to a dying world with the love and power of Jesus.

Around this time, Linda Mason took me along as a guest

speaker to a charity support group for people affected by cancer. They had agreed to let me speak without knowing the full story! When I got up I said something like, "I know this is out of order, but I am a Christian evangelist and I am here to tell you that Jesus heals today". Then I turned to the woman seated next to me. She was reliant on a walking stick and I said to her, "You are in pain, aren't you?" She agreed and I asked if I could pray for her. After prayer, all pain left her and she threw away her walking stick. Later during the meeting, she helped serve the tea and scones, carrying trays around and cleaning up—everyone was amazed!

Another lady who had been suffering with ME for 10 years was powerfully touched to the extent that she went shopping the next day, feeling the best she had felt for a good many years. God also gave me a word of knowledge for one of the ladies who had organised the meeting, and it turned out she had a damaged neck from a car accident and had been unable to move her neck freely for some years. This lady was very conservative and in a quite senior position, and I think she didn't know what to do when I slapped my hands on her neck and started praying. She told me she felt heat go through her and then she was excited to realise the pain and stiffness had disappeared and she could move her neck freely. Several people at this meeting surrendered their hearts to the Lord and many healings occurred.

One of the greatest things we witnessed during the Friday night meetings in Wishaw during this time was a young Buddhist girl giving her life to Christ. God powerfully touched her during the service.

Lindsay Raller, a 23-year-old university student from Inverness, received a profound miracle when her deformed ear canals were healed. She had been born with this problem and only had between 30 and 50 per cent hearing. Several operations had failed and, since she hated wearing hearing aids, she had learned to get by at university by making sure she sat on the front row and strained to lip-read what the lecturer was saying.

Lindsay was actually at the meeting as an usher and was helping in the prayer line. When she saw all the people getting healed, under the impulse of faith she broke ranks and pushed forward, barging through the people saying, "Pray for me, I'm deaf!".

> *"He was an alcoholic for 26 years and addicted to hard drugs ... and was instantly delivered."*

I slapped my hands on her ears and prayed, "Be healed in Jesus name!". Her ears instantly popped open and immediately she cried out, "I can hear, I can hear!" and began to weep. She cried for a long time. Her father, Tom Raller, the pastor at Inverness Assemblies of God (AOG), contacted me later and confirmed the amazing miracle God had done for her.

Another night heroin addicts came to the meeting and were delivered—they spent most of the night laid out on the floor under the power of God. Many wonderful things happened. Even the press were amazed because of what they saw.

When I laid hands on a woman who was crippled and in a wheelchair, the journalists were there to hear her cry, "I can move my feet, I haven't done that for 24 years—I feel heat in my legs!" Another lady had ringing in her ears and after I laid my hands on her ears she fell over. When she got up she said, "The ringing has gone, the ringing has gone!". The reporter was fascinated, to say the least. He interviewed Alan Watts who had been an alcoholic for 26 years, and was addicted to hard drugs, including heroin and crack, as well as cigarettes. He had been instantly delivered during a meeting three months before. The article by Rob Crilly was published in the *Aberdeen Press & Journal* under the headline "Searching for Miracles".

Alan told the story of how he used to spend his time in the world of drug addicts and the "down and out". Three months previously he had heard there was going to be a meeting but was unsure about whether to come. He had never been to church in his life—not even once! However,

Alan Watts with his mum, wife and children. I am standing to the left of Alan.

he was walking past when he heard the music and on an impulse decided to sneak in. At the moment he came through the door I was preaching about Jesus and he experienced the conviction of the Holy Spirit, came forward and gave his life to God.

The power of God touched him and he fell on the floor of the church. Alan was not only physically healed of a neck condition, he was also delivered from his long-term addiction to alcohol and drugs. Since that day he has not looked back. He was totally delivered.

His family was also a mess, but the very next day he brought his alcoholic wife to the meeting, and she was saved and delivered. On the following day, they brought their son and daughter along, and both of them got saved. By the end of the week, Alan, his mother, his wife, and their son and daughter had all received salvation and were totally delivered.

During the following week Alan turned up at the church Bible study and all the church services. In fact, he attended everything the church had going on, because he was just so hungry to learn about God. That passion hasn't changed and he is now an assistant pastor.

Some of the most powerful meetings we held during this time were at the Church of Scotland in Saline. Although this was a very traditional church, Reverend Dick Hammond had heard about the miracles and, taking a risk, invited me to come. His church had never seen anything remotely like what had been happening in our meetings.

During the first meeting, the man who was in charge of organising the church was touched by the power of God and fell to the floor. He had suffered from terrible pain in his spine and, in a moment, God healed him. The people couldn't believe it. It was a great first meeting and others also received miracles and later came to tell me in private what had happened to them. One lady was racked in agonising pain with a bad spine and two broken ribs that would not mend. Her legs were also painful and she was really suffering. After prayer she was instantly healed and her ribs were knitted together supernaturally. She slept properly for the first time in nine years and testified at the next meeting of how she was now free of pain.

The night meeting was even better. When I called people forward to give their lives to Jesus a man leapt over the pew, grabbed his crutches and began to hobble up to the front. Seeing his bandages, I asked him what was wrong and he told me that 12 months before he had fallen from a roof. Landing on the ball of his foot, he had smashed it so badly that the doctors were still unable to fix it. They had pinned

---

Sufferers "healed" by miracle worker

By Robert Scott

An arthritis sufferer, a woman with multiple sclerosis and a man who shattered his heel in an accident have told how they were "healed" in church by a miracle-worker.

Opencast mine worker Ian Hope (55) found himself discarding his walking stick and running round the church in joy after pain from a serious foot injury just disappeared … "He put his hand on my leg and prayed, 'Jesus, make this man's pain go away,' and almost immediately it did."

Excerpt from article in the Dunfermline Press, published during Dec 2000/Jan 2001.

---

the bones in his heel without success. He had been having physiotherapy but his foot was just not healing and was still swollen and sore.

I asked him to put out his foot and then put my hand over his heel and said, "In the name of Jesus, be healed!".

When I asked him how it was, he told me he could no longer feel any pain. I told him to put some weight on it and he did so and still couldn't feel any pain. When I told him to run he just threw his crutches away and ran around the church screaming.

His wife's knees had been smashed in a bad car accident many years before and as well as suffering almost constant pain she could walk only with difficulty. Running was definitely out of the question, but when she saw her husband run, she had faith to believe that she could be healed too.

"Heal me too, heal me too," she cried. I told her I couldn't heal her but Jesus certainly could, then put my hands on her damaged knees. "Run!" I told her. She started running and before you know it I had both the husband and wife running around the Church of Scotland, screaming out with joy, "I'm healed, I'm healed, I am healed!".

I am not sure that the church at Saline was quite prepared for me or for what was going on. When we first spoke, Reverend Hammond had told me meetings in their church only went for an hour. He described an occasion when a visiting African preacher had gone 15 minutes over time and the congregation became very restless and started walking out. The first meeting we held in his church went for six hours and ended up as the main story in the *Dunfermline Press.*

The following day, Dick asked me to go to Dunfermline

Hospital with him and pray for a missionary who had been told by the doctors that she was dying. During her many years of ministry in Africa she had caught an extremely rare disease. The doctors had told her she had just months to live and could do nothing to help her, so I went and laid hands on her and believed God for a miracle. (Three years later I bumped into her again and she told me that she had been totally delivered that day.)

While I was praying for her I noticed that across from me were all these sick people, so I started walking over to pray for them. Dick let me know we first had to go and get permission from the nursing sister. He told her that I was a visiting pastor from Australia and asked if we could pray for a few people in the ward who would like us to. She was happy to give us permission.

> *"She was dying from a rare African disease ... but she was totally delivered that day."*

As soon as we went back into the ward I walked over to a lady and laid hands on her. As the power of God touched her she just began to weep. I laid my hand on the head of another lady who had been sitting up in bed having a meal and as the power of God touched her, her head fell down right into her food tray! I began to pray for other people. Some cried and some fell over and all this time the nurses were trying to work out what was going on. Dick was concerned for his wife, who was waiting out in the car for him, so we eventually started heading out. As we did so the local undertaker came walking in, holding his arm and looking quite distressed. When asked what was wrong he told us he would have to give up his funeral business because he had badly injured his arm (from lifting his deceased clients). Reverend Hammond said to him, "Pastor John here has a gift of healing and he could pray for you".

I reached out and all the pain instantly left his arm. He just couldn't believe it. As I kept praying, he began to sway in the breeze and then, falling back against the wall, started to slide down it as Dick tried to stop him.

We had been so much longer than expected that Dick's wife came looking for us. She looked in surprise at Dick trying to hold up the undertaker, who was slumped over. I just couldn't help myself, so I prayed for her as well and she started bouncing up and down and shaking. This caught the attention of the hospital staff who could only look on in amazement, although one nurse came walking over to find out what on earth we were doing with the undertaker!

Wonderfully, not only was the undertaker completely healed, he also gave his life to Jesus.

Around the same time as this incredible trip to Saline, we were flying from Glasgow to London when I got talking to an older lady in the seat next to mine. I asked her if she had any sickness or pain and she told me that she had pain in her legs. As I laid hands on her she cried out, "I feel heat, I feel heat!".

I turned to the vocalists from my music team who were in the seats behind me and told them to start singing. As they lifted their voices to worship God, singing "You deserve the glory", the power of God came upon that plane and the lady in the seat across the aisle began to manifest, thrashing in her seat so much that the stewardess came rushing up to see if she was all right. At the same time, the woman sitting next to me was crying out, "What is happening? I have this strange sensation all over my body!".

The stewardess was so moved by the girls singing that she came up and asked them not to stop. We had the most incredible time on that plane and God touched the woman next to me powerfully.

During another trip we were travelling by train from Glasgow up to Inverness in the north of Scotland. The ground outside was covered with snow, it was bitingly cold and I was feeling pretty tired out. During those days we would often worship in public and in this closed train carriage I turned to Jamin, Natalie and Lynne and said, "Let's start to worship God. I feel He wants me to preach".

We began to worship and praise Him and people were turning around to see what was going on. Singing—especially praise songs—is not exactly normal behaviour on a train but it certainly got their attention! I stood up and began to share the gospel. I told them how God heals and asked if anyone wanted to give their life to Christ. A man nearby put up his hand and said, "I want to give my life to Jesus". I laid my hand on him and he prayed and received the Lord. As he did so, the power of God just came and filled up that train carriage. I will never forget that moment, as God touched that man's body, soul and spirit, changing his life forever.

Another time we were in a restaurant in Aberdeen and the girls stood up and started worshipping. As the waitress came over to see what was going on, God gave me a word of knowledge regarding her life. I spoke it out to her and she started crying. As I prayed for her the power of God touched her and she started sliding down the wall. My friend Derek was trying to hold her up and not let the other people in the restaurant see what was going on. I am sure they were left wondering!

The AOG in Scotland invited me to preach at Dunthermline and it was there that one of the most outstanding miracles I have ever seen took place, involving a lady called Helene Kelly.

As a teenager, Helene had enjoyed sport and loved to run. One day after a school race she came home complaining to her mother that her joints were aching. When it didn't improve she was eventually tested and found to have multiple sclerosis. Her condition had continually worsened until at this time, at the age of 38, her body was crippled up and she was heavily reliant on a walking frame. Chronic pain was her constant companion.

> *"I just grabbed Helene's walker and shoved it to the side."*

For 23 years she had struggled and suffered, and particularly as the mother of young children, her life was made very difficult by this terrible disease. It looked like she would soon be "graduating" to a wheelchair as her condition deteriorated.

In this desperate state, Helene hobbled painfully up to the prayer line on her walker. As I laid my hands on her and said, "In the name of Jesus, be healed", she began to shake.

In those days I was pretty wild. I used to grab walking sticks and throw them away, or take walking frames and heave them across the room. To my mind, since God was going to heal these people they obviously wouldn't need those things any longer!

I am still pretty radical, but back then I was even more so and I just grabbed Helene's walker and shoved it to the side. The power of God hit her and she fell to the floor. I just kept on praying. When I eventually stood her up and asked how she was she told me the pain had gone. I challenged her to a race and she just gave me the strangest look, so in front of the 200 odd people there that night, I pulled her along saying, "Run!" She ran all right. In fact, she ran so fast she

Helene Kelly, free after 23 years!

nearly beat me! She ran up and down the City Hall totally healed.

After the meeting, Helene was so excited she went home and got her husband and said, "Listen, we must tell everyone".

They drove to her pastor's house, because he hadn't been at the meeting that night. He was absolutely amazed and said, "We have to tell people!". He got in the car with them and they drove to another house ... and another ... and another. It was two o'clock in the morning and they were so excited by what God had done that they were knocking on people's doors and waking them up to show them firsthand God's incredible gift.

That was in November 2000 and during Christmas of that year I received a beautiful email from Helene saying something along the lines of: *"I am at home and for the first time in my life I can sit down and open presents with my children. For the first Christmas in my life, I can sit down and hold my children and play with them. Thank you."*.

Helene may have thanked me, but she also knew who she really had to thank for this incredible miracle. After her story was published in *News of the World*[31], Helene was invited to go on Radio Scotland and they asked her, "How is it you were crippled for so many years and couldn't be helped and now you are healed?".

Her simple reply was heard by hundreds of thousands of people across the nation, "It was Jesus!".

After nine months or so it was time to go back to Australia and news of what had been happening had spread that far. During our time in the UK, we saw about 1200 first time decisions for Jesus, I had prayed for an estimated

20,000 people to receive healing and preached to at least double that number. There were phenomenal miracles of every kind you could imagine. We saw cancers, tumours, growths and cysts disappear from people's bodies; people who had been crippled with ME, MS, suffered from arthritis and had paralysed limbs walked, ran and danced. People with schizophrenia, depression, fear, anxiety and suicidal thoughts were set free in their minds. Lupis, syndromes of all types, spinal conditions, stomach and eating disorders, deafness, skin and eye problems were healed.

Before we left for the USA on our way back home to Australia, we were given a farewell dinner and many of the pastors I had met and the people who had been healed were there. People who had been crippled, alcoholics and schizophrenics told their stories of how God had set them

---

Walking, running, jumping miracle
Mum crippled by MS is 'cured'

Exclusive by Rod Mills

Miracle mum Helene Kelly can romp with her kids for the first time in years – and she claims it's all down to an amazing encounter with a faith healer.

The Fife housewife was so crippled by multiple sclerosis that she used a walking stick. But now she's told how her pain was banished when she met Aussie evangelist John Mellor during this tour of Scotland. He prayed … [then] told me to walk with him and I found I could run for the first time in 10 years. It has changed my life. There has been no pain since that day …

Excerpt from article published in News of the World, Feb 2001.

---

free. It was a great celebration of God's faithfulness and I felt a strange mixture of joy and sadness. I had come to love the nation of Scotland and its wonderful people so much that it was difficult to leave. However, I knew that God wanted me to go back to Australia and see the healing power of Christ touch the people in my home land as well.

I had no idea just how amazing it was going to be!

CHAPTER FIVE

A Prodigal Returns

Jamin and I planned to spend a month ministering in the United States and Mexico on our way back to Australia and on the 17th of January, 2001, we arrived in Cameron, Missouri, to hold a series of meetings. Lynne, a member of our music team from Scotland, travelled with us.

As always, it is people's relationship with God that is most important. While many were healed, the most exciting thing about those meetings was the people who were greatly encouraged in their faith and stepped into a deeper walk with God.

A week later we were on a plane headed for Los Angeles. Seated between me and Jamin was a young lady who was travelling to Seattle to be with her dying brother. We told her who we were and then the three of us prayed together for her brother. I could sense the presence of the Lord coming on her so I asked her if she knew Jesus. She told us she was a Catholic but had never accepted that Jesus had died to pay the penalty for her sins. At 35,000 feet in the air between Kansas City and Denver she asked Jesus to be her Lord and Saviour and was powerfully touched, visibly emotional and so grateful that we had prayed for her.

I continue to be just as excited ministering to the "ones and twos" as I am at being with large congregations.

Yolanda, the Mexican lady who had been our chauffeur the first time we visited, met us at Los Angeles airport to drive us across the border.

After leaving the airport we stopped at a busy main street garage to get fuel for our long trip to Mexico and got talking to the woman running the gas station about Jesus. After walking out I looked behind me only to see Jamin and Lynne praying for this woman. She was so touched by God that she locked the garage door and requested more prayer with tears streaming down her face. Customers were outside waiting to get in to the shop and some got quite annoyed—but she was more interested in what Jesus has to offer. She was so thankful and said that God had powerfully touched her life. It's exciting to serve Jesus!

We headed to Mexico where we had arranged to minister in the San Luis prison. Unfortunately, just before our arrival there had been several murders in the men's section and we were not able to go in, although they did allow us to minister in the women's section. Many of the women were crying as Jamin and Lynne sang and as we prayed for them. Several fell over after prayer, which caused the guards some anxiety. They had never seen this happen before.

As we travelled to various churches, there were so many miracles that I can't possibly relate them all—people were healed of depression, cancer, pain—one lady had experienced a stroke 23 years before and after prayer regained much of her motor coordination. She could jump for the first time in all those years and was so excited that she just kept jumping and jumping! Another lady was suffering the results of a broken neck and all the pain left and full movement was restored.

During this time I was invited onto a Christian program called "Lift Him Up". The hosts, Tommy McWhorters and his wife, interviewed me on the show and I was also given the opportunity to preach and pray for the sick. They taped the last night of the crusade to broadcast on television—it was an awesome time to say the least.

Soon afterwards a journalist from the United Kingdom contacted me about the miracles that had been reported on the front page of the *Dunfermline Press*. He wanted to do a story for a major British paper. At this time I hadn't seen the story, but I sent him an email telling him that rather than talking to me, he should contact the people who had been healed. People must understand that Jesus is alive and that He is the One who does these marvellous things. Without Jesus nothing would happen!

On the last day I had the opportunity to lead the manager of the motel I was staying in to the Lord. She did a lot of crying as God touched her powerfully. On the flight to Australia it was the man sitting next to me and we talked about Jesus for most of our long haul to Sydney. About 30 minutes before we landed, he asked God to forgive him and accepted Jesus as his Lord and Saviour. Lynne also led the Japanese girl who was sitting next to her to the Lord—what a great trip! It was certainly an amazing time.

After a month spent ministering in the US and Mexico, I finally returned home to my native land. It was 12 months to the day since we had left. It was hard to believe all the incredible things we had seen since we flew out to Mexico, not really even knowing what we would do there.

Because of everything that had been happening, a lot of doors opened up for me when I returned to Australia. I had left an unknown pastor from the bush and I came back to a people hungry to hear what God had been doing.

The first church we ministered at was the Baptist church in Burpengary, a suburb of Brisbane. During the meeting there were many healings and miracles, as well as people committing their lives to the Lord.

> *"As I put my hand on his hunched back and started to pray, his spine began to move!"*

A lady who had been bleeding for 10 years was prayed for and became whole. The flow of blood also ceased for another woman, who had been bleeding for seven months since the birth of her last child.

A gentleman was able to close his hands for the first time in three years. A sight-impaired woman, who could only see objects as an indistinct blur, received an amazing miracle and was very excited when she could see perfectly. Another woman with double vision in one eye was also healed.

When a man whose spine was bent at a 45 degree angle came down for prayer I said to the congregation, "If you have never seen a miracle come to the front because you are going to see his spine straighten".

As I put my hand on his hunched back and started to pray, his spine began to move. People sitting up the back ran to the front of this Baptist church staring in amazement as this man slowly straightened up. God did many miracles there, some of which ended up on the front page of their local paper.

We held meetings in Caboolture and then travelled to a COC church at Woombye on the Sunshine Coast. To advertise the meetings they put a big banner up outside the building saying "John Mellor Here". That banner ended up being a signpost along the journey of my life, reminding me of just how far God had brought me.

For most of my early Christian life I sat at the back of the church, wearing an old t-shirt and shorts. I regularly argued with the pastor about doctrine and wasn't baptised in the Holy Spirit. I didn't speak in tongues and I wasn't into clapping, dancing or raising my hands. Spiritually I was just short of dead and I suffered from terrible depression.

After several years in the same church without any significant change in my attitude or condition, my pastor was naturally feeling really frustrated. He had counselled me and counselled me until in the end he felt like giving up because I was always so depressed, beat up and full of negativity. Thankfully he persevered, or I doubt that I would be where I am today!

That same pastor hadn't seen me for years. He was driving along with his wife when they noticed that big sign, outside a church of some 800 to 1000 people. Turning to his wife he said, "That couldn't possibly be the same John Mellor I knew. I am going to go tomorrow night and find out".

The very next night he came into the meeting and sat down towards the back. When the pastor announced me, he looked up and there I was; the very same John Mellor that used to sit in his church and drive him crazy! You can imagine his surprise. It just goes to show that God really does choose *"the foolish things of the world to confound the wise"!*[32] We had a really good laugh together about it.

True to His promises, God continued to do amazing miracles; just as incredible as anything that had happened in Scotland. There were people getting out of wheelchairs and blind people who had their sight restored. I prayed for a man who had a glass eye and was blind in the other. Although his glass eye didn't get miraculously transformed, God healed his blind eye and he could see again!

Another man had been in an accident 21 years before and since then his arm hung uselessly by his side as if it were dead. His hand was locked up into a fist. When I prayed for him, he was able to move his hand and bend his arm for the first time in all those years.

A reporter from the *Sunshine Coast Daily* heard about what was happening and saw it as a good opportunity to expose what he was sure was some fake fooling people. He contacted the Nambour COC church and was invited to come along to the next meeting. When he got there he went right down the front with his camera looking for a really good story to show that it was all a sham. What this journalist witnessed ended up covering the entire front-page of the next edition.

Lorraine Cottrill, a local Catholic lady, came to the meeting never imagining what was going to happen. Lorraine was crippled by MS and had braces on one leg. Parts of her legs were numb and in others she suffered terrible pain—so much so that she had just come from the pain clinic at the local hospital, although they hadn't been able to do much for her. Lorraine's husband helped her down the front to be prayed for and she was hanging onto him with all her strength, barely able to move her legs. It had been something like five years since she had been able to move her toes.

Lorraine was desperate. She had been told there were going to be miracles and she was in such a terrible state she was willing to try anything. When I prayed for her, God touched her and she fell to the floor. Then she began to scream and cry out, "I can move my toes, I can move my legs!". We got her up and took the brace off and it was the first time in over eight years that she had been able to walk

---

I saw a miracle

by Mark Furler

After 26 years crippled by multiple sclerosis, Maleny social worker Lorraine Cottrill was expecting no miracles when she went to a healing rally at Woombye this week. But she left feeling sensation in her toes for the first time in 10 years and walking without the leg brace she had depended on for six years … Twenty-four hours later she was back – still walking without her brace and still amazed at what had happened. She told me she had been almost totally numb from her waist down, especially on her left side. "Last night, for the first time for about 10 years, I felt my toes and could move my ankle." … Mrs Cottrill was so excited she spent until about 2.30am walking around her lounge room. Without the brace, her ankle would normally have rolled over, making her fall …

Excerpt from front-page article published in the Sunshine Coast Daily, March 3, 2001.

---

without a brace on her leg. The reporter was so amazed he took a photo of her and wrote an article that told how he saw a woman who was crippled and now she could walk again. The headline said, 'I saw a miracle'.

The following day, the Australian current affairs television program *Today Tonight* saw the article and their reporter contacted Pastor Chas Gullo to ask if they could bring a camera crew to Woombye COC for our next meeting and find out more. They had spoken to Lorraine and their interest was peaked by the fact that not even her doctors could explain what had happened. "We want to find out what is happening at your church," they told him.

"While the cameras were rolling she walked out, leaving her wheelchair behind!"

Chas asked me what I thought and I said to him, "Tell them to bring all the cameras in here that they want and they will see miracles happen". They got set up before the next meeting.

There is always a feeling of pressure when you are under that much scrutiny, but I know that God is the same no matter who is watching. They waited for something to happen and they weren't disappointed.

The reporter was stunned as the miracles took place in front of his eyes. One lady who had been suffering from Parkinson's disease got out of her wheelchair and all the pain left her body. While the cameras were rolling this woman walked out of the church, leaving her wheelchair behind! There were people throwing walking sticks away, blind eyes opening—incredible things happening.

Today Tonight broadcast the story on their Queensland program and the switchboard went crazy. They showed it in New South Wales, and the same thing happened. It ended up being viewed by people all over Australia. The phones were running hot with people trying to find out where I was.

It was completely weird. I had just come back from Scotland where all these amazing things had been happening, and within the first couple of weeks after I returned to Australia the same incredible miracles started manifesting. I felt like I hadn't really caught up. God is the one who made it happen. To this day I am still surprised by what He has done—and continues to do!

Today Tonight followed me to Adelaide to do another story. There, I prayed for a woman who had been paralysed and in a wheelchair for four years due to multiple sclerosis. Her legs were like dead weights and she was totally unable to move them. I laid hands on her and when the power of God came she exclaimed, "I can feel heat in my legs. For the past four years I couldn't feel anything but now I can feel heat in my legs!". I told her to start moving them. She started wiggling her toes and then slightly moving her legs. Then I said, "Start moving them up and down", and all the time I was praying for her, asking God to do a miracle. I told her to give me her hands and she said, "I can't walk". I held her hands, pulled her up and she began to walk!

When that story was broadcast, people began arriving from all over Australia. It was also televised in Asia and we had people flying in from all over the place. People just went crazy. At some of the places on my itinerary, the pastors had to take their phones off the hook because they couldn't cope with the quantity of calls.

At the COC church in Adelaide where Kevin Dales is the pastor, so many came that they couldn't fit any more people in. Eventually, Kevin had to order his staff to close and lock the big gates out the front, because it was getting so dangerous with the number of cars entering the car park and people trying to push their way into the building. That morning I had testified on local radio, and there was a massive response from callers to the station. Standing at the locked gates were people screaming and swearing at the pastors and deacons demanding to be allowed to come in. Talk about a strange situation where people abuse the pastor because he won't let them into the church!

"Father and daughter played chasings for the first time in her life!"

During this meeting Kevin's son was spectacularly healed. At 36 years old he had been through seven major spinal operations, all of which had failed and was on morphine for the pain. I prayed for him and then pulled him out of his chair, telling him to run. He wouldn't do it, so I chased him and he started running! His seven-year-old daughter had never been able to play with her dad and she asked him excitedly, "Give me a race, Daddy, give me a race!". Father and daughter ran around the car park for the first time in her life.

The next day he played "horsey" with her, galloping around with her on his back and within a few days he was moving fridges. He ended up getting a job as a concreter, something so physical it was entirely unthinkable that he would ever be able to do it—before God intervened, that is!

There were many more who God set free during this meeting. The arm of one man had been locked at a 45 degree angle for more than 20 years. His hand was also seized up as if he was making a fist. When I prayed for him in the name of Jesus both his arm and hand unlocked and straightened out.

A cancer patient was also instantly healed following prayer. The pain left her body immediately and the cancerous lumps disappeared. When doctors tested her the following week, no trace of cancer was found.

One MS sufferer had seen the program on *Today Tonight* and he immediately caught the next bus from Melbourne to Adelaide, to make it to the meeting. His faith was rewarded

This woman testified how she was healed of cancer.

as all the pain left his body and he regained the full use of his leg and arm. As he ran around the church the people clapped and cheered.

Many were healed from spinal, shoulder and neck conditions, as well as depression and arthritis. For 23 years one man had had no feeling in 50 per cent of one foot and he was totally healed, regaining full feeling and movement. The cameras caught everything as it happened.

From Adelaide we flew to North Queensland to minister at a couple of different churches.

One night a Russian-born Jewish doctor brought his daughter to the meeting. She was suffering from MS and they had flown across the world and spent thousands and thousands of dollars in many different countries trying to find a cure without success. Once again we saw the power of God push back the powers of darkness when, as we prayed, all the pain left and strength came back into her body. She walked out of the meeting normally!

Following these meetings we travelled to Katherine, to visit friends and family. It was an amazing feeling to return after everything that had happened. We held a meeting at the COC church I had pastored in, and were warmly welcomed by many old friends. During the morning service miracles occurred including the pastor's son being healed of holes in the eardrums. A lady who had been crippled by a stroke three years before got up out of her wheelchair and walked without assistance for the first time, after all the pain left her body and movement was restored to her left leg.

That evening as we ministered in the Assemblies of God Church a blind man was healed! People left the meeting carrying their walking aids over their heads like trophies.

Others were healed of Ross River fever, arthritis, depression and pain. It was a fantastic meeting!

Over the next couple of days we held meetings back in Beswick, where I again caught up with many people I knew. The flood of miracles continued; people surrendered their lives to Christ and others were delivered from alcohol addiction.

One of the greatest parts of these meetings was the worship of the aboriginal people. Jamin and Lynne were able to have a break and join in with the others. The usual camp dogs were there having the occasional fight and the drunks tried to disrupt the meeting but were brought under control. Everybody continued to worship God.

During our final week in Australia, we held meetings in Darwin at the Faith Centre. Once again we saw the power of the Lord move mightily and many were saved and healed.

People received new hips, a girl with a curved spine was healed and others received healing to their troubled minds. A lady was brought from the local hospital in a wheelchair, still wearing her hospital nightie and with a nametag strapped to her wrist. Her leg was dreadfully swollen and she was in a lot of pain. After prayer all the pain left her and, healed, she walked out without assistance while her friend wheeled the empty chair from the building.

The next night another lady was brought from the hospital. She had crippled, painful legs and was hobbling on a walking stick. It wasn't long before she threw the stick away and walked normally with no pain. Both these ladies were discharged from the hospital and kept coming to the meetings, which were to be our final ones in Australia. So many great things happened it is impossible to share it all.

We were excited at the thought of returning to Scotland and seeing God continue to move.

When the time finally came for us to leave, my son Joel joined us. It was wonderful to have two of my children with me. From then on, Joel's responsibility was to take photographs and record miracles.

On the trip back to Scotland we stopped off at Brunei for a couple of days where we witnessed about Jesus to some Moslems and met members of the underground church. Around the middle of April 2001, we finally returned to Scotland. As soon as I arrived Rod Mills and other reporters began asking if I had more stories for their newspapers.

Within a couple of days Jamin, Joel and Lynne went off to a youth camp at Brighton. It felt strange to be without them after all this time. I found it much easier to have their help and support and by the time they returned I was overcome with weariness. Eventually I booked tickets for me and Joel to go to La Palma in the Canary Islands for a week. It was a rest I badly needed. Thankfully, as we were always on a tight budget, it turned out to be a very low cost place to visit. Food in particular was very cheap. Unfortunately, our dreams of swimming in the ocean and relaxing on the sand were dashed when we discovered that it was very common for people to sunbake and swim in the nude! We decided to stay well away from those areas of the beach and instead spent our days climbing the beautiful sand dunes or wandering around the town and relaxing.

It was great to spend time with Joel after a year apart from him and on the last day I finally started to feel like I was winding down.

The next day we got up at 4am to catch a flight to

Edinburgh. Starting the following evening, we held a series of three night meetings at the Edinburgh Apostolic Church as guests of Pastor Ron Goulton. Hundreds came and there were many miracles. Each night I prayed for hours so that no-one would miss out. The meetings finished in the very early hours of the morning.

Over the three nights, at least seven cripples walked without their sticks, crutches, and walkers after prayer. A 29-year-old lady called Alice Riddell also received a miracle. Alice had been born with flat feet, a painful condition, and had worn corrective shoes for most of her life. She couldn't dance and at times found it difficult to even walk. Alice had been to a number of meetings and each night when she had come forward for prayer, nothing had happened.

On this particular night, there were about 100 to 150 people out the front waiting for me to pray for them. When I finally came to Alice she was in tears and so desperate to be healed that she had taken off her corrective shoes. She was crying out to God with everything she had, as she stood there in pain, having waited for about an hour by this time. She told me the pain in her feet was excruciating.

I bent down and put my hands on her feet, which were vividly encased in a pair of red socks, and after praying for her a couple of times, I commanded the arches to grow. As I turned away, Alice cried out and grabbed me, squealing delightedly, "Look at my feet, look at my feet!".

There was no doubt she had definite arches. That was early in 2001 and Alice Riddell has not worn corrective shoes since that night. Soon afterwards she was dancing in church.

A couple of days later we were back at Wishaw for our usual Friday night meeting. About half of the people who attended had come because of a story in the *News of the World* [33].

One interesting thing about these meetings was that they drew a lot of New Age healers involved in reiki, crystals and spiritualism. The gods they serve are not able to help these people and they came and found out first-hand the reality of the power of Jesus Christ.

Early in May I went to Germany for a week on my own, leaving Joel and Jamin in Wishaw to help Crawford and Sheila with the church. Although I felt peace at this decision, it was difficult being on my own and I felt lonely and sad. Being alone caused me to start thinking about the past and how much I missed being with Joy and the children. Thankfully, as I talked with God the pain eased and I sensed His peace.

Mum No. 2 is cured by miracle…

Exclusive by Rod Mills

A Scots doctor who was so ill she didn't even have strength to watch TV has told how she was miraculously cured …

… Linda Mason was forced to give up work when she contracted ME, also known as Chronic Fatigue Syndrome.

The condition left her so exhausted [she] couldn't even read a book and had to spend most of her days lying in bed. But Linda, who was a GP before her shattering illness, says her symptoms have disappeared after just two healing sessions with Australian pastor John. And the day after her second visit, [she] was so full of beans she swam 14 lengths and joined a gym!

Dr Alec Workman said, *"… when she came to me after the meeting with Mr Mellor, she had undergone a transformation… She seems completely cured."*

Excerpt from article published in News of the World, April 22, 2001.

Dieter, the local pastor, took me to Dachau, the Nazi concentration camp where so many Jews and other innocent people perished during the Second World War. There are no words to adequately describe what I saw there. The gallows, the gas chambers ... there were photos on display and even actual footage of the camp. It was a very emotional visit to say the least and a sobering reminder of how low human beings can sink without God.

We had many fantastic meetings over the week that I was in Germany and saw many people get healed.

On my return to Scotland we went straight out onto the streets witnessing. We had a really good meeting at Grove COC. A deadly brain tumour had crippled one young lady who hobbled into the service on a walking stick. When I asked her if she knew Jesus I discovered she was angry with God for all her suffering. As I took her walking stick I told her, "You are about to see how good God is". After I prayed all the pain left her body, strength returned to her legs and to her surprise she was able to walk normally. The pain that had been her constant companion for six agonising years was gone and she was so excited she gave her life to Jesus.

"The pain that had been her constant companion for six agonising years was gone!"

From Grove we travelled to France, Belgium and Holland, before returning to Scotland via England.

Back in Wishaw a few weeks later, many unsaved people came to the meetings after reading the newspaper article about Dr Linda Mason's healing from chronic fatigue syndrome. A number of people who needed to use walking sticks were healed of their infirmities and able to walk out without their sticks. A language teacher was healed of ME: all the pain left her body and the Lord touched her in a powerful way. There were great miracles: pain leaving bodies and cripples walking.

At the Sunday night meeting, a man came from the Baptist church in Buckie who was very sceptical. He came up to the front because he was concerned about a friend of his who had been prayed for and had fallen over. As he was trying to help her up, I asked him if he needed prayer. His first response was, "No, I'm all right". Then he thought about it and remembered he was wearing glasses. "All right, you can pray for my eyes", he said somewhat reluctantly.

I took his glasses off and put my thumbs on his eyes, asking God to heal him. He fell backwards on the floor and when he got back up off the ground, he could see perfectly

Dr Linda Mason is shown here on the far right.

clearly. No more glasses! He came back the next night and apologised, saying, "I never believed it was possible and [thought] you were pushing people over. I felt an intense heat go through my eyes and then when I got up everything was clear!". What an amazing testimony!

In the middle of June we went to France for a week and again we saw God do some incredible things. Many people were healed as well as saved but I think the miracle that touched my heart the most concerned a couple who had been told they couldn't have children. They had only been married for three years and the doctor had told the husband it would take a miracle for them to have a child because it was totally impossible. They had come to me when I was in France a month earlier and we had prayed together that she would conceive and have a child despite what the doctors had told her. We had joined hands as I prayed, "In the name of Jesus, I decree a miracle, I command this woman to conceive, I command the problem in the husband to be healed and rectified". Of course, during my visit I prayed for many people and I had forgotten all about praying for them until I returned to France this time and the couple came up to me. They were so excited and told me they had received the news just four days before. She had conceived within several days of that time of prayer the last time I was in France. It's exciting what God can do!

Another outstanding thing happened during a street outreach event we took part in near the beach in Dunkirk. Lynne and Jamin were singing together with some members of the church we were visiting and I was asked to preach; thousands of people were walking up and down. I started preaching about Jesus and asked if anyone would like to give their lives to God. When I asked if anyone would like prayer for pain, several ladies came up. One lady had just had an operation; she had pain all through her body, in her legs and stomach. We were out in the open and there were people everywhere watching this. I took her by the hands and said, "In the name of Jesus I command all pain to leave this body". She started to get excited as she realised she could move her legs and was without pain. She testified to the public who were milling around. Another lady came up who had pain in her back as well as other parts of her body and I prayed for her. I am unsure whether she was completely healed but she felt incredible relief from the pain and she also gave her life to Jesus. Everybody began laughing when she testified in French, "I thank you for the wonderful massage".

The following night a man came to the meeting and gave his life to the Lord. He had heard me preaching in the street the night before and told us how the words he heard touched his heart powerfully, and he knew he had to give his life to Jesus.

Overall, I think the most amazing thing is this. During our previous visit to France, I had known people were being healed but because I don't understand the language very well I wasn't really sure what was going on. This time I asked people who had been healed during our previous meetings to come up and testify and we had quite a few people respond who I wasn't even aware of. It was very encouraging. God always does so much more than what we are aware of!

Late in June we held a couple of mid-week meetings in Newtongrange Community Church, Scotland. The church there was very expectant and had spent time beforehand praying and fasting. They were looking for God to move with power—and He did! The meetings were packed both nights and we saw amazing miracles, but the most dramatic happened on the Thursday night to a lady called Shuna Munro, whose daughter had brought her to the meeting. I found out later that Shuna was against the church and wanted nothing to do with God but she was so ill she had agreed to come.

Shuna was suffering from many chronic illnesses, including arthritis, diabetes and psoriasis, which had caused a rash down her neck and across her head as well as different parts of her body. She shuffled painfully into the meeting, leaning heavily on a walking stick, and could hardly speak because one of her health problems had damaged her voice. When she came through the door I said to her, "Tonight you are going to receive a miracle". As people often do, she just gave me a strange look!

After I had preached I called Shuna up, complete with

God has saved me!

by Shuna Munro

He has saved me! He has given me my life back. I was crippled with arthritis for about eight years and had to use a walking stick. I came to Newtongrange on 28th June and gave my life to the Lord and he gave me back life!!

I had a big lump under my tongue, which made it difficult to talk – he removed it. I was healed of seven ailments altogether; my eyes, mouth, throat, my back had lumps all over it, psoriasis, diabetes and rheumatoid arthritis. My body straightened and I actually grew an inch! My back was awfully stooped before – I actually changed shape …

An excerpt from Shuna Munro's personal testimony.

---

walking stick, and when I prayed for her she fell to the floor and was instantly delivered. She got up and all the pain was gone—she couldn't believe it. That night she ran, she danced—all without her walking stick. New skin formed on her neck in front of our eyes and the terrible rash disappeared. All the scabs were falling from her hair and she was delivered from seven different ailments, including having to wear glasses! Shuna told me she had a 17-year-old son, Hamish, who had been incapacitated by arthritis for the last five years. I told her that if she brought him along to the next meeting, God would deliver him.

By the end of the night Shuna was not only dancing with me around the room, but much more importantly, had given her life to Jesus.

On the following Sunday night she brought Hamish to the meeting at Leigh Baptist Church. When I asked who would like to give their lives to God, Hamish was the first one out. He came hobbling out on his walking stick, which I took from him and threw onto the floor. When I prayed for him he fell to the ground and like his mother he was totally healed. His crooked fingers straightened and all the pain left his body. He just couldn't believe it—he was totally healed. I received a report several days later saying that he had been going to give up playing the bagpipes but now that his fingers were straightened playing wasn't a problem any more. His condition had been so bad that to play with the band he had to go in a wheelchair. God did some wonderful things in that family. The next time Hamish entered a bagpipe contest, he won and no-one could believe that he was marching along with the other bagpipe players, straight and tall, instead of being pushed in a wheelchair. When he went up to receive his award he testified that the greatest thing wasn't that God had healed his body, but that Jesus had saved his soul. He had found Jesus and been born again. He unashamedly testified to everyone there about his new found faith in Jesus.

Back in Peterhead I heard that a lady who had been powerfully healed in a meeting we had held the year before was in hospital with heart problems and they asked me to go and pray for her.

The nurses at Peterhead Hospital had heard how this woman had received a miracle and had thrown away her walking stick because she was no longer crippled, so when I went in to pray for her, I was asked to pray for another lady who was paralysed and in a wheelchair. They warned me that

---

Faith healer gets crippled piper Hamish walking again …

Exclusive by Rod Mills

A Scots teenager crippled by arthritis has made a miracle recovery after being cured by amazing faith healer John Mellor.

Talented Hamish Munro, 17, was a schoolboy bagpipe champion until he was struck down by the disease five years ago and confined to a wheelchair.

Hamish … suffered a second devastating blow when the doctors told him he was suffering from epilepsy. He was forced to take a daily cocktail of drugs to help ease the harrowing symptoms of both conditions. But Hamish has now confounded doctors by taking up his pipes and rejoining his marching band after one session with the Australian faith healer …

Excerpt from an article published in News of the World, September 23, 2001.

---

time was short as this woman had a physiotherapy session booked.

The physiotherapist and the nursing sister were both there and I discovered that this lady had MS and this terrible disease had crippled her until she was stuck in a wheelchair and without hope.

I turned to the hospital staff and said to them, "You know it was amazing what happened in that meeting to that lady who is in the next ward". The physiotherapist told me that she wasn't sure she believed in "all of that". I just laid my hands on this lady and began to pray for her and said to her, "Listen, it is easy for God to get you out of that wheelchair, but the greatest thing you need is to give your life to Jesus". I asked her if she would like to do that and right there in front of the hospital staff she received the Lord. Then I told her, "Now God is going to touch you".

As I prayed for her legs and put my hand on her head, she said suddenly, "I feel heat, I feel heat." Heat was going through her legs where she hadn't been able to feel much sensation for some time. "Well, get up and walk!", I said to her. When she told me she couldn't, I took her by the hands and pulled her out of her chair. All of a sudden she started taking steps. The nursing staff and the physiotherapist were in an uproar, "How did you do that? How did you do that?" they were asking, half-excited and half-frightened. I turned to them and said, "It was Jesus—simply the Name of Jesus".

CHAPTER SIX

Challenges & Triumphs

On the fourth of July we flew down to England to go to Brighton, Eastbourne and Bournemouth churches and about a week later, travelled to a village called Bunessan, on the remote Scottish island of Mull. The people there had never seen the miracle working power of God before. Bunessan has a population of about 100 people, and on the night of our first meeting, about half of that population turned up to witness astounding miracles. They watched in awe as cripples walked and the oppressed were delivered. One lady had been reliant on a walking stick for 15 years, and had been in terrible pain for 30. She was dramatically delivered and couldn't believe it when all the pain left her body and she no longer needed her walking stick. Ian Grainger, the retired Church of Scotland minister who had organised the meetings, was due for a knee replacement and could scarcely sleep because the pain in his ruined knee was so intense. Ian received a miracle and ended up running up and down the stage. The people had never seen anyone falling over under the power of the Holy Spirit and were astonished when they fell on the floor after prayer. A large proportion of the village ended up being splayed out across the hall. It was an amazing sight. The next day the whole village was abuzz talking about the previous night's events. Many gave their lives to the Lord, including one young man who was a practising Buddhist.

In the town of Tobermory the following night, I prayed for a lady who was crippled with MS. Her balance was almost completely gone, her legs were numb and she was hobbling on a stick with her husband propping her up. When I asked them if they would give their lives to Jesus, they declined. I then prayed for the woman after taking her stick from her and she fell over. After praying for her again I pulled her up and she walked without assistance. It was obvious the strength was back in her legs. I said to her, "Tomorrow you'll have to buy some jogging shoes". The husband later told me, "If I see her run tomorrow then I will give my life to God". I told him there was no waiting for tomorrow, as I turned to his wife and said, "... try and catch me!" She proceeded to chase me around the front of the church to the amazement of all who were there. Both the husband and wife then gave their hearts to Jesus!

> *"With my own eyes I saw the legs of a man born with cerebral palsy stretch and straighten!"*

We travelled back to the mainland to Kilmartin as the guests of the Church of Scotland there. So many amazing things occurred that I couldn't possibly recount them all. But one story that must be told is that of another Hamish. This Hamish had suffered from cerebral palsy since birth. It affected the left side of his body, and although he had learnt to live with his disability, his balance was affected and he had never been able to walk or run normally. What happened that night was vividly described by Rev Alison Ross, who said:

"In Kilmartin we saw amazing miracles, arthritic pain gone in an instant, new knees, ME healed, pain and disability from cancer removed, alcoholics delivered, demons shown the door, but with my own eyes I saw the legs of a man born with cerebral palsy, stretch and straighten as John prayed, his spine too, straightened and wasted muscle strengthened. This man, who had never run IN HIS LIFE (46 years) ran round the church and then later asked John if he could run again, it felt so good. His face was aglow, his friends were amazed … best of all he said "thank you God," and now he's telling everyone all about it. John believes that God has a call on this man's life. His

Hamish runs for the first time in his life.

name is Hamish, watch this space!!

… Healing, recommitment, conversion, deliverance, oppression lifted, laughter and tears, praise and worship, and then late on the Sunday night, for about an hour, a small group of us were privileged to share a special moment with God. We were dancing, singing a new song, filled with joy and simply worshipping our God who makes all this possible, who does the impossible and uses us to do it. The wind is blowing again, the wind is blowing again, just like the day of Pentecost, the wind is blowing again!!!"

Ian Hair, who had been spectacularly healed of ME at a meeting in Wishaw four months before after being drawn to the meetings by an article in the *News of the World*, brought his sick mother forward so I could pray for her. She had trigeminal neuralgia—a condition that results in pain so terrible, it has been described as among the most acute known to mankind[34]. Ian's mother couldn't believe it when the pain left her body. God is so good!

An Indian man from Glasgow named Gurmit was set free of painful "frozen shoulders" and was amazed after receiving prayer that his arms were free from pain and had recovered full mobility. His sister, Sheila, brought him along—she had been dramatically healed of serious cancer of the bladder 14 months previously at Wishaw. Our Lord is so awesome! So many miracles happened over that weekend that there isn't time to tell it all. Jesus is so wonderful!

And yet the greatest miracle of all was that many people surrendered their lives to Christ or recommitted their lives to Him.

Shortly afterwards, on Mull, a lady called Anne Ross testified about what happened to her friend, Mary Frances

Jones, at the meetings last time we were in Kilmartin. This is what she shared:

"Mary Frances had had a brain tumour for five years and despite having three operations it kept coming back. The last time she came she was deciding whether to go in for another operation because it was about the size of an egg and pressing on to the back of her eye. She also had back problems as a result of a fall about three years before and was on morphine because the pain was so bad and the doctors couldn't do anything for her. She needed a stick to help her walk and decided to come to the meeting.

Mary got up on the stage and John prayed for her and the pain in her back went. Before that she had been sitting on the seat and going from side to side because it was so painful just to sit there. She couldn't lie on her back for any length of time—if at all. After John had prayed for her she put her stick in her bag

"... the scan had come back and there was no sign of a tumour!"

and she was sitting on the pew (you know how hard pews are) and she was wriggling and couldn't believe the pain had gone— and it had! John prayed for her a few times after that for the brain tumour that she had.

Mary was going home the next day; that night when she was getting in and out of the car it was as if she was two years old compared to the way she was when we were driving up to the meeting and the next day the pain still wasn't there! She was absolutely DELIGHTED. She went home to Wales and [when I] phoned her up to see how she was doing, the pain still hadn't *returned. She had to go and get a scan to see if the tumour was still there because she had to decide if she was going in for another operation. About a fortnight later Mary phoned [me up] in tears; the scan had come back and there was no tumour—no sign of a tumour whatsoever. The doctor said they would do a second scan just in case they hadn't seen it (even though it had been the size of an egg!)—there was no doubt whatsoever that there had been an egg-sized tumour before she received prayer.*

She had the second scan done and was called up to the surgery to discuss the results. The doctor said, "Sorry, but we can't find a tumour anywhere!". They tried to explain it away by saying that she had been on chemotherapy—but the fact is that she had been receiving chemo for a long time and the tumour just kept increasing in size—and the doctors confirmed

Mary Frances Jones—healed of a brain tumour after the doctors had given her just months to live.

this. Because tumours can move about your body, Mary asked for a full body scan which revealed that there is absolutely nothing there! She still wasn't convinced so asked for it in writing because her family wouldn't believe her that the tumour had gone. Her back is still ok—in fact she was getting withdrawal symptoms because she's off the morphine now and she's starting to accept that she actually has a life now! She is over the moon …"

There are so many more true stories I could tell of what God did during that time (and has continued to do since), but as it says in John 21:25: *"And there are also many other things which Jesus did, the which, if they should be written every one, I suppose that even the world itself could not contain the books that should be written."*

> *"Joel had come with us to record miracles … after five months he was burnt out!"*

Joel had come with us to record miracles and take photos. He did a fantastic job but was so busy that after five months on the road he was burnt out and couldn't do it anymore! The flood of miracles was so incredible. Exhausted, Joel ended up taking a position with a church in Brighton.

Late in July we travelled down to Stanstead in London to hold a meeting in Bishop Storton. Soon after arriving we went down the main street inviting people and putting up posters. I really enjoyed it and spent hours talking to people about Jesus. We invited many sick people to come to the meeting.

One couple I invited received an incredible miracle. The wife had been suffering from MS for 23 years and when I prayed for her Jesus totally healed her. The place was in an uproar. More importantly, both her and her husband committed their lives to the Lord.

Jamin, Joel and I went from there to the COC Conference in Brighton. It was a good chance to catch up with the Australian COC leadership and share about what had been happening. During the conference they ordained me as an evangelist. God had really turned things around since I left Katherine.

We spent a few weeks in Brighton, doing a lot of walking and praying and just generally relaxing. It was wonderful.

In the middle of August I went to Spain. The first week was pure relaxation and when I finally preached in the local church I realised it was the first time I had done so for four weeks!

The next day my hosts took me to the airport. Unfortunately, I had mixed up the time of my flight and instead of 3.20pm it was actually 3.20am! Needless to say, I was exhausted by the time my flight actually left, and very glad to finally make it back to Brighton. After catching up with Joel I returned to Wishaw. It felt like coming home.

Within a couple of days things were back into full swing and I was preaching every night.

One of the first places I went to was an apostolic church in Edinburgh, where a woman called Jean Ferrier was so desperate to be touched by God she arrived very early and sat on the front steps for hours. While I had been travelling, Jean, who was a deacon in her church, had attended a conference where Rev Alison Ross told the story of how

Hamish had been healed from cerebral palsy. For years Jean had been crippled with a terrible nerve condition and other afflictions and she made up her mind that if I was preaching somewhere near where she lived she would go to the meeting.

When Jean heard there was going to be a meeting in Edinburgh, she decided to catch a train there and with a friend, arrived about 2pm. With nowhere else to go, they got to the steps of the church an hour or two later. The meeting wasn't due to start until 7pm but Jean was willing to wait.

She was so desperate for a miracle and the doctors had given her no hope of her condition ever improving.

"... as I took her by the hand, she began to run around the church, totally healed."

I can still remember that as I was preaching that night, God healed people with eye conditions, ear conditions, pain and all kinds of things. Jean was sitting on the front row because she had arrived so early and I walked over to her, laid my hands on her and began to pray. Although I wasn't too sure what was wrong she was obviously in pain and I had seen her walking sticks. The power of God flowed through her and when I told her to run, she fell to the floor! I got her up and again told her to run. This time, as I took her by the hand, she began to run around the church, totally healed. It was an incredible miracle.

Later, Jean told me how risky it had been for her and her friend to come to the meeting. Not only had the two women had to travel a great distance which was very difficult because she was so ill, they had to spend hours waiting for the meeting to start. After the meeting they had to get back home and the area they lived in was very, very rough. There is no way people would normally catch a train there in the middle of the night as it was just not safe, but that is what these women did, walking back from the train station through the dangerous neighbourhood to their homes.

But God rewards simple faith. Jean shared her testimony of healing in Troon in 2006—she is still totally healed. She has been on a number of mission trips to Romania and no-one would even know she had been crippled unless she told them. Our God is certainly incredible!

> *"... no one would even know she had been crippled unless she told them!"*

In that same meeting, there was a young man in his early twenties who was half-blind because of a disease in his eyes. His uncle had been healed in one of our meetings and had encouraged him to come. The young man was a chef but he was losing his eyesight. The disease had already caused his vision to be blurred. He and his mother were two of the first people to come out the front in response to the gospel message. I prayed for his eyes and nothing happened. Then again, and still nothing happened. After praying for him six or seven times there was still no change in his condition. I told him to wait and said that I would come back and pray for him again later. There were hundreds of people who had come forward and it was much later before I made my way back to where he had been and realised he was still there. It was about 12.45am and he had been standing there for literally hours. I had been praying so intensely for other people that I hadn't realised he was still waiting. This time when I laid my hands on his eyes he told me that his eyes felt funny, but "kind of better". I prayed again and when he opened his eyes he had perfectly clear vision. His mother cried as her son pointed things out, looking at things he could not see before. God restored his vision. What a wonderful God we serve!

One night in Edinburgh a reporter from *The Scotsman,* Scotland's national newspaper, came to the meeting. The power of God was so strong in that meeting that I only had to wave my hand and people fell over. It was incredible. The meeting went until 2am. Not much later than usual!

A few days later, the article appeared in the full colour supplement of the paper. To my shock, my photo covered the entire front page with a headline that reads *"Hands on— Can John Mellor really heal through faith alone?"* A double page spread described the meeting through the eyes of the reporter.

I sat in the train that day hiding my face behind a paper hoping that no-one would recognise me.

The date was September 11, 2001, and everything else was to be overshadowed for some time to come by one of the most awful tragedies the world has ever seen. It was a day that none of us will forget …

Soon afterwards we took our first trip to Bulgaria and it was one of those weeks that make me wonder if I am the only person who gets themselves into impossibly crazy situations!

The flight to Sofia, the capital of Bulgaria, took just

three and a half hours, but the drive to Plovdiv seemed to take forever and we only just arrived in time for the meeting. By now I had been wearing the same clothes for about 24 hours. It was very hot in Plovdiv and I was exhausted, sweaty, hungry and unshaven. Even worse, I desperately needed to go to the toilet! I had thought we would go to a hotel to get ready but the pastor wanted me to go and preach as soon as I got out of the car. There was nowhere to get changed except behind a wall in the pastor's office, so I pulled my crumpled clothes out of my bag, quickly got changed and went in to the meeting.

It wasn't long before people began to get healed and in their eagerness, the crowd of about 200 surged forward, grabbing us and pushing us up against the back wall. All Jamin and I could do is pray our way out! People were falling over in the spirit with no-one to provide support. The whole thing was totally crazy. After about four hours I was a complete wreck.

Totally exhausted, I was desperately looking forward to having a rest either at the pastor's house or in a hotel. When I got outside there was a car running and ready to go and I saw that Jamin was already sitting in the back next to two strange women. A man was driving and another woman was in the front passenger seat.

To my horror, instead of a short drive to our accommodation, we just kept driving and driving. I tried to find out where we were going. The woman in the front could speak just a few words of very broken English and when I asked her where we were headed all she could say was Shumen. Thinking it was a suburb of Sofia, I questioned her again, only to discover it was a town on the other side of

Bulgaria, near the Black Sea! It turned out the two women in the back were socialists and incredibly anti-Christian. Their next destination was Shumen so they had commandeered a place in the vehicle.

Jamin and I were incredibly squashed and uncomfortable in the back seat. One of the women had fallen asleep and was half collapsed on top of me and the other one spent the whole trip telling me how she hated Americans and spewing out a whole lot of party propaganda!

As soon as we arrived in Shumen I crawled, exhausted, into a bed at someone's house only to find out when I woke up that there had obviously been previous occupants. We were off to a great start but things could only get better.

During the meeting that night, a woman who had come from another church got offended because I didn't pray for her quickly enough

"They were socialists and had commandeered a place in the vehicle."

and started telling the people on the front line not to listen to me. She was calling out, "Come here, come here. Don't listen to him!". It was the last thing I needed, particularly when I couldn't speak the language. The missionary who was hosting us didn't speak Bulgarian and the interpreter hardly spoke English, so we were at this woman's mercy. In addition, there was no music team, just a man with most of his fingers missing who had been asked to play the piano! But, you know, God has a sense of humour, and despite all these challenges, miracles happened and six people gave their lives to the Lord.

After the meeting we returned to the same accommodation. Before going to sleep I wrapped myself in a coat and put an old shirt over my head to protect myself from the pillow, praying against any bed bugs.

The next morning we got up early and drove back across Bulgaria. We held an incredible meeting back in the church at Plovdiv that night. The power of the Holy Spirit was so strong virtually everyone we prayed for was healed. The translator told me later that the next day one lady woke up to find that a huge growth, which had been the size of a man's hand, had disappeared.

That night we had about four or five hours sleep and I woke up feeling like a zombie only to discover that the pastor had organised for me to go to people's homes and pray for them. I was so tired I was sick. Everything ached and I felt delirious.

At each place, as we prayed for people more kept appearing. It was as if they were coming out of the woodwork. When they found out I was praying for someone, all the neighbours would run down and get me to pray for them too. I love the people but I have to tell you I don't know if I have ever felt so tired.

From Povliv we travelled by plane to Gatwick, where we picked up some luggage I had left behind on one of our trips (this is such a common occurrence it has become a standing joke). Then it was off by bus to Heathrow so we could fly to Sao Paulo, Brazil.

Amarillo, the pastor in Sao Paulo really looked after us and I managed to squeeze in a much-needed nap before we were driven to a city about one and a half hours away for a night meeting. About 400 people turned up and the place was packed. I was so tired I was concerned that I was becoming delirious. Although my head was spinning and my vision blurred, as soon as I got up to preach the anointing came on me and I was fine.

That night, for the first time in my life, I fell asleep while standing in front of a man, praying for him. One minute I was praying, the next I was asleep, slumped on top of him in exhaustion. Thankfully, after that interesting experience, I had enough sense to sit down and leave Jamin and the other pastors to pray for the sick!

The service went for about four or five hours and afterwards we had great fellowship and more food. My head was really swimming by now and I had broken the exhaustion barrier to a whole new level. I felt stoned. In the middle of the night I finally fell into a fitful sleep.

"One minute I was praying, the next I was asleep, slumped on top of him in exhaustion."

The next day I woke up early after just three hours sleep. My whole body felt weird. We drove to another city to hold a meeting. Our host's driving style was wild but I was so tired I no longer cared!

After a couple of days we travelled to Santiago, Chile, where we met up with Freddy Bartolo, a pastor I had known in Queensland, who took us to the city of Vina de Mar. Virtually as soon as we arrived I collapsed. Hours later when Freddy tried to wake me up to get ready for the meeting he was unable to get a response and he ended up having to take the meeting. I slept like the dead for eight hours straight.

From there we went to La Florida and then on to Talca where we held a fantastic meeting in the city hall. The meeting on the following night was even better. About 600 turned up and 50 people were saved. God is so faithful. One lady who came forward for prayer had been in agony for many years. She had to be helped into the building, leaning heavily on a walking stick. The first time I prayed for her not much happened. The second time, the pain began to go. The third time, I told her to bend over and Freddy turned to me in concern, saying, "You can't ask her to bend over". [He knew what I didn't, that the doctors had fused her spine with a steel rod and she could not bend.] I got angry and replied, "Tell her to bend over now". She bent over and was totally healed. When she stood back up she had no pain and full flexibility in her spine.

> *"Her spine had been fused with a steel rod ... but when she stood up she had full flexibility!"*

That incredible miracle happened towards the end of 2001 and was further evidence that there is no limit to what God can do if we make ourselves available to Him. I cannot begin to describe how grateful I am to have seen—and continue to see on a daily basis—His power at work in the lives of people like you and me.

* * * * *

The story of the many miracles that have happened in the years since then will hopefully be told another time. In the meantime, Jamin and I ended up staying in Chile much longer than expected. It was during this period that I met the woman who was to become my wife.

Erika and her sister attended a church that we ministered at, and after seeing her for the first time I couldn't stop thinking about her. Without knowing each other very well it wasn't long before we married. The next step was to work on getting a visa for Erika to return to Australia with me.

Unfortunately, nothing about this was as easy as I had hoped and we spent months trying to get everything in place for us to return home. Even more unfortunately, it wasn't long before the cracks in our relationship began to show. Erika couldn't speak English and although my Spanish rapidly improved we often misunderstood each other. To say we had a cultural clash of mammoth proportions is an understatement. We did finally make it to Australia but sadly our relationship didn't improve. We travelled together for months, visiting England and Scotland and many other places. No matter what happened things didn't get better.

For more than four years we tried to make it work. I based myself in Chile and travelled alone as Erika no longer wanted to join me, returning whenever I could. During this time I continued to see incredible miracles and healings, and lives turned to Jesus. The ministry God had called me to continued, but it was more difficult and I felt the strain of our troubled marriage continuously, longing for things to be different.

I did everything I could think of; prayed, fasted, sought counsel, cried out to God. But in the end our marriage was over. I was devastated, and yet at some level also relieved at the lifting of the terrible pressure we had both felt.

I thank God for my pastor, Chas Gullo, who worked with me through this terrible time and continues to provide wise counsel and oversight, both for me as a man who wants above all else to live a life that is pleasing to God, and for the ministry God has given me.

* * * * *

Despite the disappointment and sorrow, God has been—and continues to be—so faithful.

CHAPTER SEVEN

His Goodness Never Ends

L ooking back through what I have written, it all seems to have happened so fast. By necessity, telling this story has been like skipping from treetop to treetop but underneath it all there are also many stories that have not been told. While many are joyful stories of healing and miracles there are also stories of those who haven't yet received all they are hoping for. And for me, while these years have been filled with so much that has been amazing, there have also been many challenges.

Everything that has happened since my early days as a Christian has certainly taught me a lot. I have had wonderful times and I have had difficult times, moments when I have been so worn out I feel as if I have nothing left to give. I have walked through the agony of broken relationships and every day I continue to walk through the reality of those tragedies. Many times as I have travelled I have longed for my own bed in my own home, to have some normality in my life rather than what seems to be never-ending change.

Some people think that travelling the world is a

wonderful life. It is certainly a novelty for a while and can be interesting and exciting, but it can also be exhausting. It is not uncommon for me to sleep in seven different beds in one week. I can be in four different countries in one day. In my bag I carry about eight different types of currency. I continually find myself in strange, uncomfortable and even dangerous situations, and realise just how inadequate I am without God.

On just one of these many occasions, I travelled all day on a bus from Brighton to Stansted Airport feeling really tired and worn out from preaching. When I got off the bus I grabbed my bag and a local pastor picked me up. He dropped me at my accommodation and was to return in an hour and a half to take me to the meeting. When he had gone I opened my bag to take out my clothes, only to find it was full of women's underwear and dresses! Thinking to myself, "I can't preach in these clothes!", I rang the pastor in a panic and cried, "Help!". He kindly loaned me his suit but the only problem was he was tall and lean. The suit coat sleeve hung halfway down my hand and the trousers dragged under my heel. I felt very awkward in his clothes but incredibly grateful not to be wearing a dress!

To get my bag back, I ended up having to fly to Rome to swap bags in the airport with the other bag's owner.

A similar incident happened just two weeks later. I arrived at Luton airport and the same pastor picked me up and dropped me at my accommodation. When I opened up my bag to get ready I discovered to my embarrassment that, once again, it wasn't mine! You can imagine how I felt about having to call and tell him what had happened. This time I was rushed to Stansted airport and caught the bag's owner with just minutes to spare before he caught a flight to Germany!

Many times I have woken up in the middle of the night with no idea where I am, or have got up out of bed to turn the light switch on only to find it is not where I thought it was. On other occasions I have been picked up from the airport and fallen asleep in the car only to wake up in shock, having forgotten that I was in another country.

Different cultures, different food, customs, languages—it is continual change without end.

There are challenges to living a life like this. But even though there is a price to pay, with it comes a great joy and a satisfaction I know I couldn't find anywhere else. The more you sacrifice out of love for Jesus and obedience to His will, the more you find your life. With Him the world takes on greater meaning and becomes full of incredible possibilities.

Looking back, I can see that the times when I have experienced the most bitter suffering are also the times when I have grown the most in my relationship with God. And those times have always involved making a decision whether to continue with God or whether to deny His plan for my life. While sometimes that decision has seemed so hard, living life God's way cannot be compared with doing it on my own. I could not walk away. I choose not to, no matter what happens. I am in love with Him and have been spoiled forever. There is nowhere else to go! This life isn't always easy, but every time you come to that crossroads you have to choose whether to take the easier path, or to continue living according to God's plan. The alternate path might not necessarily be a way of sin, but it is an "easier" way. The price of following Him can seem extremely high at times;

financially, physically and emotionally. It can cost you in ways you never imagined and you can experience great highs but also incredible lows. However, the peace that God gives you is almost too wonderful to describe.

I have always had a sense of God's purpose in my life, right from when I first came into relationship with Him; a deep sense that He has called me to be an evangelist. Even when I didn't know the meaning of that term, I wanted to reach out to others with the gospel. Because of that, I had a hunger to read books about the old-time evangelists, preachers like D.L. Moody, Charles Finney, John Wesley, C.C. Studd, Billy Graham and Billy Sunday. I read the biographies of these men who gave their lives to serve God.

I dreamt of preaching to thousands like Billy Graham and D.L. Moody and it drove me. It took years for God to take the dust of my life and turn it into something that could be used for His glory and I certainly don't pretend to have it all together—far from it. I am not about to pretend that there are no challenges in my life. But this I know—my God is faithful beyond our comprehension. When He says He will never leave you or forsake you,[35] He means it! No matter what you face—whether good times or difficult times—He walks beside you.

I never cease to be amazed at all God has done and continues to do, and I hope I never will be. And no matter how tired I feel at times, there is one thing that continues to spur me on and that is the overwhelming love of God for every individual life. When I see someone suffering, whether physically or emotionally, my heart fills with the need to let them know that there is a God in heaven who loves them more than they may ever comprehend and who has the answers they need. God's love stirs me to want to reach out and tell people that there is hope of so much more.

The miracles and healings God has done are incredible, but the greatest miracle of all continues to be His power to change the lives of ordinary people. I have experienced it profoundly in my own life as God has taken my fractured life and used it for His purposes. Despite my many failings and mistakes—despite the fact that I am so far from the type of person I would choose if I was God, He continues to love me and to use me.

I could tell you hundreds, if not thousands, of true stories about how God's power, love and forgiveness have changed people's lives. One of these I related to you in Chapter Four, in the story of Alan Watts, who was delivered from long-term alcoholism and a serious addiction to hard drugs, including heroin and crack cocaine. Within a short period of time Alan's wife, two children and his mum also came into relationship with God. They continue to love and serve God today. This entire family was turned around from profound dysfunction into a shining trophy of God's goodness.

Another transformed life that stands out to me is that of Grant Gibson. When Grant and I met in Scotland, he had been out of work for years because he was totally unable to hold down a job. His wife had left him a few years before and he had just hit the drink. At that time Grant had spent the past five months in bed, drinking himself into oblivion and was in the deepest depression.

Grant's brother-in-law was a spiritualist who wanted to help him and he tried getting him to attend spiritualist meetings, thankfully without success. As someone who was attracted to spiritual things, when he heard about the meetings we were holding, he decided to see if he could get Grant to go along.

They had a plan to go to the meeting and afterwards go out drinking together, but instead Grant came forward to receive Jesus. When I laid hands on him the power of God struck him and he fell to the floor of the church, shaking. Since that day he hasn't had a drink. Just like Alan, he had a hunger and thirst for God from day one, grew very quickly and his life has been totally transformed.

After a while Grant met and married Patricia. It wasn't long before God provided him with a good job and after three years, he was made the assistant pastor of the church at Wishaw. At the time of writing this book he is still there, faithful right-hand man to the pastor. He went from five months in bed as a semi-alcoholic in the deepest depression, to becoming a true man of God, who is hard working, reliable and faithful.

God works differently with different people, but no matter how He chooses to work, His love and mercy are always the same. Both Alan and Grant were almost instantly changed, but for some the path is different and may be much longer. It certainly has been for me; much longer! At times it can seem like the pain, anxiety and trouble is never going to end. But no matter what challenges you face, when you hold on to God, you will eventually win through.

Despite the challenges of my life, when I grasped hold of that truth, things began to change. I began to change. I developed such an awareness of God's presence that now I have no doubt He is with me all the time. That knowledge gives me a great sense of His peace. When I go into a meeting, I feel confident because **I know He is with me**. I feel confident that miracles will happen, not because of who I am, but because of who He is.

He is a miracle working God.

I see myself as an ordinary Aussie bloke and I think most other people view me that way as well, but I have no doubt at all that God is exactly who the Bible says He is.

There is no formula—to Christianity, to life, to ministry or even to miracles. It is all about relationship. When I have gone through intense suffering I have always sought to go deeper in God and not get bitter and angry. I have had dry seasons in my Christian life but I have never been able to get away from that love I have for God, although I wonder how He puts up with me sometimes!

All the intense suffering and disappointment in my life—God has turned into something wonderful. Without those difficulties, I don't know if I would be where I am now. I don't know if I would have seen what I have seen.

There is no striving. It is so real, so simple—like God has taken me back to being a trusting child, after living as a cynic for so many years. Now I just simply believe and obey. And what I want more than anything else is for people to come into relationship with Christ, understanding the truth of all He is.

The most important thing to realise is that the needs you have are so much more than just physical needs. Often people come to meetings with pain, sickness or depression, and they are looking for relief, but one of the very first things I do is begin to make people aware of their great need for salvation. Real salvation is to receive forgiveness for your sins, real salvation is to receive Christ and to believe in Him and accept the gift of eternal life. The main goal I have is to preach the full message of salvation, that God can come into your life and you can be born again and transformed by His power. You can have a new life in Christ, you can have eternal life in heaven with Him but you can also have physical healing. Whatever your need, He is the God who is there and He is willing to touch your life and set you free.

The main theme of the Bible is salvation, but most people think salvation is only about God forgiving us for living life our own way instead of His, and giving us eternal life in heaven with Him after our physical bodies die. Incredible as that gift is, salvation encompasses so much more. One of the Greek words translated in the Bible as "save" is the word *sozo,* which as well as saving people from their sins means to *make whole and to heal*[36]. It is this word that is used in Matthew 1:21 where it says:

"And she will have a son, and you are to name him Jesus, for he will save his people from their sins."

Salvation encompasses not only the forgiveness of sins, but also physical and emotional healing. Healing and salvation go together, and all of this is waiting for you. More importantly, God is waiting for you and has been since time began. There is nothing about you He doesn't already know, no matter how intimate, yet He loves you more than life itself.

As the writer of Psalm 139 said:

"For you created my inmost being;
you knit me together in my mother's womb.
I praise you because I am fearfully and wonderfully made;
your works are wonderful,
I know that full well.

My frame was not hidden from you
when I was made in the secret place.
When I was woven together in the depths of the earth,
your eyes saw my unformed body.
All the days ordained for me
were written in your book
before one of them came to be." [37]

These words are just as true for your life as they were for the writer of that psalm. That same God who created you is longing for you to know Him the way He knows you.

I hope that through this book you have seen what God can do with even the most broken of lives. But most of all, that the God I serve, the God of the Bible, truly is the Saviour of the world.

www.johnmellor.org

Notes

Foreword

[1] John 14:12, NIV.

[2] Luke 9:2, NKJV.

[3] Mark 16:18, NKJV.

Introduction

[4] *Today Tonight* is a current affairs program in Australia.

Chapter 1

[5] Darwin is the capital of the Northern Territory.

[6] The Australian government pay every family with children a small supplemental allowance.

[7] The details of this story were told to me by Joe Wilson some years ago.

[8] A billabong is a water hole. A common definition is that a billabong is formed when the U-bend in a river is cut off, separating itself from the rest of the river. The billabong may stay wet even after the river itself has dried out.

[9] A billy is a tin container used over a fire to boil tea when you're camping in the outback.

[10] Crocodiles use the "death roll" to drown their victims, by rolling over and over them in the water. Once their prey is dead, they will lodge the corpse under a rocky outcrop or a fallen log and leave it there for a week or so until it is ready for eating.

[11] Flying Doctor is short for the Royal Flying Doctor Service—an aero medical health service for those who live, work or travel in outback and regional Australia.

[12] An Esky is an ice-box or cooler.

[13] Pronounced "Nooka".

[14] Bulldust is fine dust with a consistency like talcum powder. It is created when the ground dries up after rain or flood and then breaks up. It is common in the outback.

[15] Clap sticks are two pieces of shaped wood which are clapped together to make sounds during ceremonies.

[16] The didgeridoo, another traditional instrument, is made from limbs or tree trunks hollowed out by termites (insects).

[17] It is an aboriginal tradition in the Walpiri nation (a particular aboriginal people group) that every person at the funeral has to lay on the body of the dead person. As this is not allowed in towns where by law they must bury their dead in coffins, each person lies on the coffin instead, irrespective of how young or old they are. Some might not conduct the full ceremony, but instead just lay briefly on the coffin.

Chapter 2

[18] The dingo is native to Australia and generally lives in family packs. They do not bark but instead have a distinctive howl, which can be very eery at night in the outback.

[19] While all tribal aboriginals still hold their ceremonies, such as corroborees, only a few are still involved in "pointing the bone" and other related practices.

[20] A goanna (pronounced go-anna), is an Australian native reptile. They are a species of monitor lizard and grow to about 160cms in length.

[21] Cursed.

[22] The flood waters eventually rose to over 18 metres. 3600 people were left homeless and 5000 were evacuated. www.ema.gov.au (disasters database).

[23] A "poddy calf" is a calf that has been raised by hand-feeding.

[24] Cockatoos and galahs are Australian native birds.

[25] Matthew 22:14, NKJV.

Chapter 3

[26] The story of Barbara Downie was published in a full page article by Michelle Gallagher in the *Wishaw Press* headlined, "Is Wishaw new pilgrim place?". Margaret Neely's testimony was also mentioned in this article.

[27] Lupus is a chronic inflammatory disease that impacts the auto-immune system. It can effect various parts of the body, especially the skin, joints, blood and kidneys.

Chapter 4

[28] The term "faith healers" is used here to refer to those who identify themselves as spiritual healers, and operate outside the teachings of the Bible. This includes those involved in the New Age movement, and/or who use channelling, past lives and other regression techniques amongst others. These people usually charge a fee for their services. This is very prevalent in the UK.

[29] *News of the World, The Scotsman, Press & Journal* all published major stories on what God was doing in Scotland.

[30'] Myalgic encephalopathy (ME) is also known as chronic fatigue syndrome. It is a chronic, fluctuating disease whose most common symptoms are severe fatigue or exhaustion, problems with memory and concentration and muscle pain.

[31] The article referred to was written by Rod Mills and published in February 2001. It was the first of three articles written by Rod on miracles that occurred during our ministry in Scotland.

Chapter 5

[32] Corinthians 1:27, KJV.

[33] *News of the World* is Britain's biggest newspaper. At the time the story was published, it was reaching five million people per week.

Chapter 6

[34] Trigeminal neuralgia is a disorder of the trigeminal nerve, the fifth and largest cranial nerve. TN produces excruciating, lightning strikes of facial pain, typically near the nose, lips, eyes or ears. www.tna-support.org

Chapter 7

[35] Hebrews 13:5, NKJV.

[36] Strong's Concordance, used via www.blueletterbible.org

[37] Psalm 139:13-16, NIV.